**ULTIMATE M**
**GLORY ST. GERMAIN /**

Edited by Shelagh McKibbon-U'Ren RMT UMTC

# ADVANCED RUDIMENTS
# ANSWER BOOK

# UltimateMusicTheory.com

ISBN: 978-0-9813101-8-3

# ULTIMATE MUSIC THEORY: *The Way to Score Success!*

## The Ultimate Music Theory workbooks are for all Musicians.

The more we understand the universal language of music, the more we are capable of communicating our ideas through performing and writing music, interpreting musical compositions of others, and developing a deeper appreciation of music. It is through music education that we progress from student to musician and are able to enjoy and understand music at a more comprehensive level.

### Acknowledgements
Dedicated with love and gratitude to my husband Ray for his encouragement, and to our children Chrystal, Catherine, Ray Jr., David Joseph, Sherry Rose and our grandchildren, for their inspiration.

Published in 2011 by Gloryland Publishing
First printing - 2008. Revised edition - 2011.
Printed in Canada.
GlorylandPublishing.com

Library and Archives Canada Cataloguing in Publication St. Germain, Glory 1953-
Ultimate Music Theory Series / Glory St. Germain

### Gloryland Publishing - Ultimate Music Theory Series:
| | | |
|---|---|---|
| GP - UP1 | ISBN: 978-0-9809556-6-8 | Ultimate Prep 1 Rudiments |
| GP - UP1A | ISBN: 978-0-9809556-9-9 | Ultimate Prep 1 Rudiments Answer Book |
| GP - UP2 | ISBN: 978-0-9809556-7-5 | Ultimate Prep 2 Rudiments |
| GP - UP2A | ISBN: 978-0-9813101-0-7 | Ultimate Prep 2 Rudiments Answer Book |
| GP- UBR | ISBN: 978-0-9813101-3-8 | Ultimate Basic Rudiments |
| GP - UBRA | ISBN: 978-0-9813101-4-5 | Ultimate Basic Answer Book |
| GP - UIR | ISBN: 978-0-9813101-5-2 | Ultimate Intermediate Rudiments |
| GP - UIRA | ISBN: 978-0-9813101-6-9 | Ultimate Intermediate Answer Book |
| GP - UAR | ISBN: 978-0-9813101-7-6 | Ultimate Advanced Rudiments |
| GP - UARA | ISBN: 978-0-9813101-8-3 | Ultimate Advanced Answer Book |
| GP - UCR | ISBN: 978-0-9813101-1-4 | Ultimate Complete Rudiments |
| GP - UCRA | ISBN: 978-0-9813101-2-1 | Ultimate Complete Answer Book |

# Table of Contents

**Ultimate Music Theory Guide - Advanced**

**Score: 60 - 69** Pass; **70 - 79** Honors; **80 - 89** First Class Honors; **90 - 100** First Class Honors with Distinction

## Ultimate Music Theory: *The Way to Score Success!*

# ULTIMATE MUSIC THEORY: *The Way to Score Success!*

The focus of the **Ultimate Music Theory** Series is to simplify complex concepts and show the relativity of these concepts with practical application. These workbooks are designed to help teachers and students discover the excitement and benefits of a music theory education.

Ultimate Music Theory workbooks are based on a proven approach to the study of music theory that follows these **4** Ultimate Music Theory Learning Principles:

- ♪ **Simplicity of Learning** - easy to understand instructions, examples and exercises.

- ♪ **Memory Joggers** - tips for all learning styles including auditory, visual and tactile.

- ♪ **Tie it All Together** - helping musicians understand the universal language of music.

- ♪ **Make it Relevant** - applying theoretical concepts to pedagogical studies.

---

These workbooks help students prepare for
nationally recognized theory examinations including
**The Royal Conservatory™ of Music**
and the
**Carnegie Hall Royal Conservatory The Achievement Program™**

---

The Ultimate Music Theory Series includes these EXCLUSIVE BONUS features:

- ♪ **80 Ultimate Music Theory Flashcards** - Vocabulary, Musical Signs, Rhythm and more! Use the Flashcards at the back of the book to study the Musical Terms. Each side contains a term in **bold**. The definition is in the square box on the opposite side of the Flashcard.

- ♪ **Ultimate Music Theory Guide & Chart** - convenient summarization to review concepts.

- ♪ **12 Comprehensive Review Tests** - support retention of concepts learned in previous lessons.

- ♪ **Web Support** - free downloadable materials for teachers and students.

- ♪ **Ultimate Music Theory Monthly Newsletters - sign up for FREE.**

- ♫ **Note:** Each "♫ Note" points out important information and handy memory tips.

- ♫ **Note:** The convenient and easy to use Ultimate Music Theory Answer Books match the student workbooks and are available for all levels.

 UltimateMusicTheory.com

# Lesson 1        C Clefs - Alto and Tenor

**C CLEFS** - the **ALTO** Clef and the **TENOR** Clef.

Different Clef Signs may be used to establish the placement of Middle C based upon the range of the voice or instrument. The following shows the placement of Middle C in the Treble, Bass and 5 C Clefs.

Treble      Soprano     Mezzo-Soprano    Alto       Tenor       Baritone     Bass

The **ALTO** Clef is drawn with the arrow pointing to the **THIRD** line → indicating **MIDDLE C**.

The **TENOR** Clef is drawn with the arrow pointing to the **FOURTH** line → indicating **MIDDLE C**.

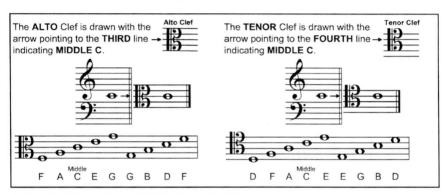

1. Draw the following clefs and Middle C on each staff.

**TREBLE CLEF**      **ALTO CLEF**      **TENOR CLEF**      **BASS CLEF**

Middle C      Middle C      Middle C      Middle C

2. Name the following notes in the Alto Clef.

Middle C   D   E   F   G   C   B   A   G   F

3. Name the following notes in the Tenor Clef.

Middle C   D   E   F   G   C   B   A   G   F

## THE CIRCLE of FIFTHS

The **CIRCLE OF FIFTHS** is a map of the Major and minor Key Signatures. It identifies the flats and sharps found in each key. The number on the Circle of Fifths indicates how many flats or sharps are in the Key Signature. The Major Keys are written on the **OUTSIDE** of the circle and the relative minor keys are written on the **INSIDE** of the circle.

♫ **Note:** The reason it is called the Circle of Fifths is the distance between each key (when moving clockwise) is five letter names. (An interval of a Perfect Fifth.)

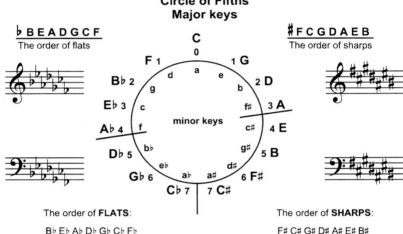

The order of **FLATS**:

B♭ E♭ A♭ D♭ G♭ C♭ F♭

**B**attle **E**nds **A**nd **D**own **G**oes **C**harles **F**ather

The order of **SHARPS**:

F♯ C♯ G♯ D♯ A♯ E♯ B♯

**F**ather **C**harles **G**oes **D**own **A**nd **E**nds **B**attle

♫ **Note:** Always write the flats and sharps in the correct order.

1. Copy the order of flats and sharps in the Alto Clef.

2. Copy the order of flats and sharps in the Tenor Clef.

## WRITING THE CIRCLE of FIFTHS

When **WRITING THE CIRCLE OF FIFTHS,** use UPPER case letters for Major keys OUTSIDE the circle and lower case letters for relative minor keys INSIDE the circle.

Complete the Circle of Fifths:
1. Write the order of flats on the top left and the order of sharps on the top right.
2. Write the Major Keys on the **OUTSIDE** of the circle. Start with **F** Major and move clockwise:
   F, C, G, D, A, E, B. Then repeat the order again: F♯, C♯, C♭, G♭, D♭, A♭, E♭, B♭ (UPPER case).

♫ **Note:** Use the sentence Father Charles Goes Down And Ends Battle.

3. Draw the landmark line under the A♭ and under the A.
4. Write the minor keys on the **INSIDE** of the circle. Start with **f** minor (relative of A♭ Major) and move clockwise: f, c, g, d, a, e, b. Then repeat the order again: f♯, c♯, g♯, d♯, a♯, a♭, e♭, b♭ (lower case).

# Circle of Fifths

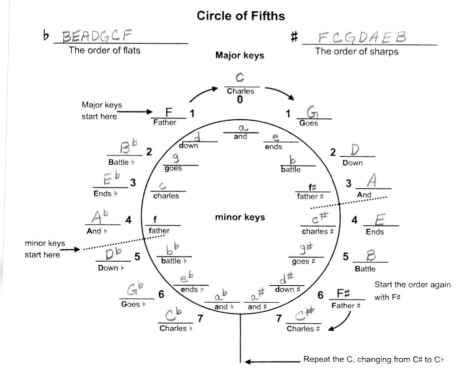

♭ _BEADGCF_
The order of flats

Major keys

♯ _FCGDAEB_
The order of sharps

♫ **Note:** Major keys and their relative minor keys are three semitones (three letter names) apart.

7

## ALTO CLEF - NOTES and KEY SIGNATURES

1. Rewrite the following notes at the same pitch in the Alto Clef. Name the notes.

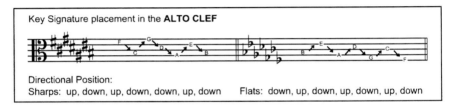

<u>C</u>  <u>F</u>  <u>A</u>  <u>E</u>  <u>B</u>  <u>G</u>  <u>B</u>    <u>C</u>  <u>A</u>  <u>E</u>  <u>D</u>  <u>D</u>  <u>G</u>  <u>F</u>

♫ **Note:** The sharps and flats in the Key Signature for the Alto Clef are placed in the SAME directional position as in the Key Signatures for the Treble Clef and Bass Clef.

---

Key Signature placement in the **ALTO CLEF**

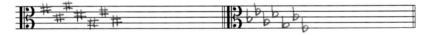

Directional Position:
Sharps: up, down, up, down, down, up, down    Flats: down, up, down, up, down, up, down

---

2. Copy the above Key Signature placement in the Alto Clef below.

3. Write the following Key Signatures in the Alto Clef.

   G Major    F♯ Major    D Major    E Major    C♯ Major    A Major    B Major

   F Major    A♭ Major    G♭ Major    B♭ Major    D♭ Major    E♭ Major    C♭ Major

## TENOR CLEF - NOTES and KEY SIGNATURES

1. Rewrite the following notes at the same pitch in the Tenor Clef. Name the notes.

C   G   D   B   A   A   F        C   F   B   D   G   E   C

♫ **Note:** The sharps and flats in the Key Signature for the Tenor Clef are placed in the same directional position as the FLATS in the Tenor Clef, Treble Clef and Bass Clef.

Key Signature placement written in the **TENOR CLEF**

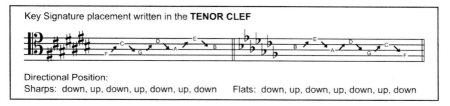

Directional Position:
Sharps: down, up, down, up, down, up, down     Flats: down, up, down, up, down, up, down

2. Copy the above Key Signature placement in the Tenor Clef below.

3. Write the following Key Signatures in the Tenor Clef.

G Major     F♯ Major     D Major     E Major     C♯ Major     A Major     B Major

F Major     A♭ Major     G♭ Major     B♭ Major     D♭ Major     E♭ Major     C♭ Major

## WRITING SCALES in the ALTO CLEF and TENOR CLEF

When **WRITING SCALES** in the **ALTO CLEF** and **TENOR CLEF**, always place the Key Signature in the correct position on the staff.

♫ **Note:** Scales may be written WITH or WITHOUT a center bar line. A center bar line CANCELS all accidentals but NOT the Key Signature.

1. Write the following scales, ascending and descending. Use the correct Key Signature. Use whole notes.

   a) A flat Major in the Alto Clef
   b) a sharp minor harmonic in the Tenor Clef
   c) b flat minor melodic in the Alto Clef
   d) E Major in the Tenor Clef
   e) f sharp minor natural in the Alto Clef
   f) c minor melodic in the Tenor Clef

a)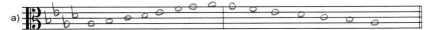

b)

c)

d)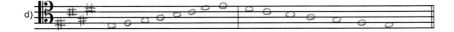

e)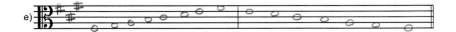

f)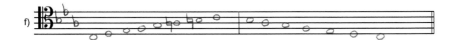

## ITALIAN, FRENCH and GERMAN TERMS

**TERMS** are written directions given by a composer to the musician for performance of a piece of music. Terms or signs are usually written in **Italian**, but can also be written in **French**, **German** or **English**.

### Italian Terms and Signs    Definition

**Dynamics**

| Term | Definition |
|---|---|
| *crescendo, cresc.* | becoming louder |
| *decrescendo, decresc.* | becoming softer |
| *diminuendo, dim.* | becoming softer |
| *forte, f* | loud |
| *fortepiano, fp* | loud then suddenly soft |
| *fortissimo, ff* | very loud |
| *mezzo forte, mf* | moderately loud |
| *mezzo piano, mp* | moderately soft |
| *piano, p* | soft |
| *pianissimo, pp* | very soft |
| *sforzando, sf, sfz* | a sudden strong accent of a single note or chord |

1. Write the Italian term for each of the following definitions.

| *mezzo forte, mf* | *fortepiano, fp* | *sforzando, sf, sfz* | *diminuendo* *decrescendo* |
|---|---|---|---|
| moderately loud | loud then suddenly soft | a sudden strong accent | becoming softer |

### French Term    Definition

| Term | Definition |
|---|---|
| *cédez* | yield; hold the tempo back |
| *léger* | light; lightly |
| *lentement* | slowly |
| *modéré* | at a moderate tempo |
| *mouvement* | tempo; motion |
| *vite* | fast |

2. Write the French term for each of the following definitions.

| *mouvement* | *léger* | *vite* | *lentement* | *modéré* |
|---|---|---|---|---|
| tempo; motion | light; lightly | fast | slowly | a moderate tempo |

### German Term    Definition

| Term | Definition |
|---|---|
| *bewegt* | moving |
| *langsam* | slow, slowly |
| *mässig* | moderate, moderately |
| *mit Ausdruck* | with expression |
| *sehr* | very |
| *schnell* | fast |

3. Write the German term for each of the following definitions.

| *mit Ausdruck* | *sehr* | *schnell* | *langsam* | *mässig* |
|---|---|---|---|---|
| with expression | very | fast | slow, slowly | moderate |

## RHYTHM - BASIC BEAT and PULSE

**BASIC BEAT**: TOP number of the Time Signature indicates how many Basic Beats in a measure. BOTTOM number of the Time Signature indicates what type of note equals one Basic Beat.

**PULSE**: where the rhythmic emphasis falls. Simple Time Pulse: **S** = Strong **w** = weak **M** = Medium
Compound Dotted Pulse: **S·** = Sww **w·** = Mww **M·** = Mww

In Compound Time each group of 3 Basic Beats equals one DOTTED Basic Beat. (Compound B.B.)
In Compound Time each group of 3 pulses (Sww or Mww) equals one DOTTED pulse. (S·, w·, or M·)

A **PLUS** (+) sign indicates to join pulses into one rest; a **TILDE** sign (~) indicates to NOT join pulses.

1. Add rests below each bracket. Cross off the Basic Beat (and Compound B.B.) as each beat is completed.

12

## ADDING RESTS in SIMPLE TIME and COMPOUND TIME

When **ADDING RESTS** in **SIMPLE TIME** and **COMPOUND TIME**:

A Strong pulse joins a weak pulse into one rest.

A Medium pulse joins a weak pulse into one rest.

A weak pulse CANNOT be joined to a Medium or a weak pulse.

A weak pulse **ALWAYS** stands alone.

| Simple Time | Compound Time |
|---|---|
| S + w | S · + w · |
| M + w | M · + w · |
| w ~ M | w · ~ M · |
| w ~ w | w · ~ w · |

1. Write the Basic Beat, pulse and Compound Basic Beat (when necessary) below each measure. Add rests below each bracket to complete the measure. Cross off the Basic Beat (and the Compound Basic Beat) as each beat is completed.

## Lesson 1　　　　Review Test

Write the Circle of Fifths on a blank piece of paper. Use it as a reference while writing the review test.

**1.** a) Name the following intervals.

10

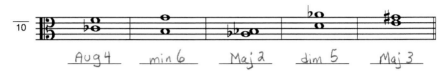

　　　Aug 4　　　min 6　　　Maj 2　　　dim 5　　　Maj 3

b) Invert the above intervals in the Treble Clef. Use whole notes. Name the inversions.

　　　dim 5　　　Maj 3　　　min 7　　　Aug 4　　　min 6

**2.** For each of the following Dominant triads, name:
a) the correct key (Major or minor).
b) the position (root, 1st inversion or 2nd inversion).

10

a)　　e minor　　f minor　　D Major　　F Major　　a minor

b)　　root　　1st inv　　2nd inv　　2nd inv　　1st inv

**3.** For each of the following triads, name:
a) the Root.
b) the type/quality (Major or minor).

10

a)　　F　　Bb　　C　　D　　B

b)　　Major　　minor　　minor　　Major　　minor

14

4. Name the key of the following melody.

    a) Transpose the given melody **UP** a minor sixth in the Treble Clef. Use the correct Key Signature. Name the new key.

    b) Rewrite the given melody at the **SAME PITCH** in the Alto Clef. Use the correct Key Signature.

___
10

Key: B♭ Major

a) Key: G♭ Major

b)

5. Write the Basic Beat and the pulse below each measure. Add rests below each bracket to complete the measure. Cross off the Basic Beat as each beat is completed.

___
10

15

**6.** Write the following scales, ascending and descending. Use the correct **KEY SIGNATURE**. Use whole notes.

10

a) Tonic minor, melodic form, of G Major in the Alto Clef
b) b flat minor harmonic in the Tenor Clef
c) enharmonic Major of C sharp Major in the Alto Clef
d) E Major in the Tenor Clef
e) relative minor, natural form, of F sharp Major in the Alto Clef
f) g sharp minor melodic in the Tenor Clef

a)

b)
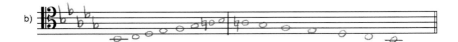

c)
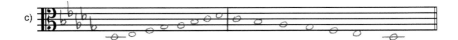

d)
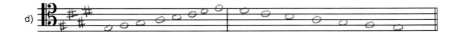

e)
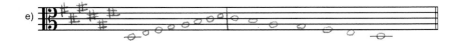

f)
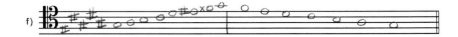

7. For each of the following cadences, name:
   a) the key and chord symbols (V-I, iv-i, I-V, etc.).
   b) the type (Perfect, Plagal or Imperfect).

10

a) E Major  IV  V    a) Bb Major  II  I    a) e minor  i  V
b) Imperfect         b) Plagal            b) Imperfect

8. For each of the following melodies:
   a) name the key.
   b) add the correct Time Signature directly on the music below the bracket.

10

Key: E Major

Key: b minor

Key: Db Major

Key: d# minor

17

**9.** Match each musical term with its English definition. (Not all definitions will be used.)

| Term | | Definition | |
|------|------|------|------|
| *bewegt* | b | a) | with expression |
| *sehr* | i | b) | moving |
| *léger* | g f | c) | sweet, gentle |
| *cédez* | | d) | at a moderate tempo |
| *diminuendo, dim.* | j | e) | slowly |
| *mit Ausdruck* | a | f) | yield; hold the tempo back |
| *modéré* | d | g) | light; lightly |
| *mouvement* | h | h) | tempo; motion |
| *vite* | k | i) | very |
| *lentement* | e | j) | becoming softer |
| | | k) | fast |

<sub>10</sub>

**10.** Analyze the following piece of music by answering the questions below.

<sub>10</sub>

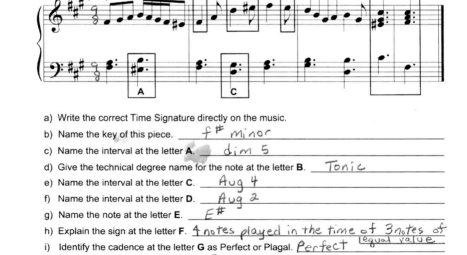

**Schnell**                                                                 S. McKibbon

a) Write the correct Time Signature directly on the music.

b) Name the key of this piece. ___f# minor___

c) Name the interval at the letter **A**. ___dim 5___

d) Give the technical degree name for the note at the letter **B**. ___Tonic___

e) Name the interval at the letter **C**. ___Aug 4___

f) Name the interval at the letter **D**. ___Aug 2___

g) Name the note at the letter **E**. ___E#___

h) Explain the sign at the letter **F**. ___4 notes played in the time of 3 notes of equal value___

i) Identify the cadence at the letter **G** as Perfect or Plagal. ___Perfect___

j) Explain the meaning of **Schnell**. ___fast___

18

# Lesson 2    Scales - Technical Degrees

**SCALES** may begin on any degree (note) of the scale. **TECHNICAL DEGREE NAMES** are used to identify each degree of a scale. Scales may be written with or without a center bar line.

1. Write the technical degree name for each degree of the scale.

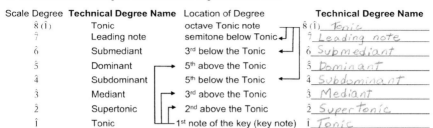

| Scale Degree | Technical Degree Name | Location of Degree | Technical Degree Name |
|---|---|---|---|
| $\hat{8}$ ($\hat{1}$) | Tonic | octave Tonic note | $\hat{8}$ ($\hat{1}$) _Tonic_ |
| $\hat{7}$ | Leading note | semitone below Tonic | $\hat{7}$ _Leading note_ |
| $\hat{6}$ | Submediant | 3rd below the Tonic | $\hat{6}$ _Submediant_ |
| $\hat{5}$ | Dominant | 5th above the Tonic | $\hat{5}$ _Dominant_ |
| $\hat{4}$ | Subdominant | 5th below the Tonic | $\hat{4}$ _Subdominant_ |
| $\hat{3}$ | Mediant | 3rd above the Tonic | $\hat{3}$ _Mediant_ |
| $\hat{2}$ | Supertonic | 2nd above the Tonic | $\hat{2}$ _Supertonic_ |
| $\hat{1}$ | Tonic | 1st note of the key (key note) | $\hat{1}$ _Tonic_ |

♪ **Note:** When writing a scale, begin and end on the same technical degree. A **circumflex** " ˆ " or **caret** sign (hat) above a number ( $\hat{3}$ ) indicates the degree number of the scale.

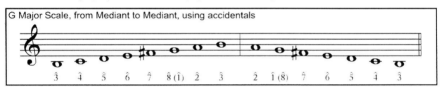

G Major Scale, from Mediant to Mediant, using accidentals

2. Write the following scales, ascending and descending, using accidentals. Use whole notes.

a) D Major Scale, from Mediant to Mediant, in the Alto Clef

b) B flat Major Scale, from Dominant to Dominant, in the Treble Clef

c) E Major Scale, from Submediant to Submediant, in the Tenor Clef

## HARMONIC MINOR SCALES

A **HARMONIC MINOR SCALE** will use an accidental for the raised 7th note (the Leading note). When writing a harmonic minor scale starting on a scale degree other than the Tonic note, the raised 7th note ( ↑$\hat{7}$ ) is counted UP from the TONIC and not from the first note written for the scale.

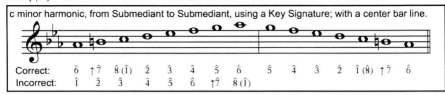

c minor harmonic, from Submediant to Submediant, using a Key Signature; with a center bar line.

| Correct: | $\hat{6}$ | ↑$\hat{7}$ | $\hat{8}(\hat{1})$ | $\hat{2}$ | $\hat{3}$ | $\hat{4}$ | $\hat{5}$ | $\hat{6}$ | $\hat{5}$ | $\hat{4}$ | $\hat{3}$ | $\hat{2}$ | $\hat{1}(\hat{8})$ | ↑$\hat{7}$ | $\hat{6}$ |
| Incorrect: | $\hat{1}$ | $\hat{2}$ | $\hat{3}$ | $\hat{4}$ | $\hat{5}$ | $\hat{6}$ | ↑$\hat{7}$ | $\hat{8}(\hat{1})$ | | | | | | | |

♫ **Note:** When writing a harmonic minor scale beginning on the LEADING NOTE, an accidental is required for the raised 7th note ( ↑$\hat{7}$ ) for BOTH the lower and upper Leading note.

1. Write the following harmonic minor scales, ascending and descending, using a Key Signature. Use whole notes. Write the scale degree number below each note.

   a) f sharp minor harmonic, from Leading note to Leading note, in the Treble Clef

   ↑$\hat{7}$  $\hat{8}(\hat{1})$  $\hat{2}$  $\hat{3}$  $\hat{4}$  $\hat{5}$  $\hat{6}$  ↑$\hat{7}$   $\hat{6}$  $\hat{5}$  $\hat{4}$  $\hat{3}$  $\hat{2}$  $\hat{1}(\hat{8})$  ↑$\hat{7}$

   b) g minor harmonic, from Supertonic to Supertonic, in the Alto Clef

   $\hat{2}$  $\hat{3}$  $\hat{4}$  $\hat{5}$  $\hat{6}$↑$\hat{7}$  $\hat{8}(\hat{1})$  $\hat{2}$  $\hat{1}(\hat{8})$↑$\hat{7}$  $\hat{6}$  $\hat{5}$  $\hat{4}$  $\hat{3}$  $\hat{2}$

   c) a minor harmonic, from Subdominant to Subdominant, in the Tenor Clef

   $\hat{4}$  $\hat{5}$  $\hat{6}$↑$\hat{7}$  $\hat{8}(\hat{1})$  $\hat{2}$  $\hat{3}$  $\hat{4}$   $\hat{3}$  $\hat{2}$  $\hat{1}(\hat{8})$↑$\hat{7}$  $\hat{6}$  $\hat{5}$  $\hat{4}$

   d) b flat minor harmonic, from Mediant to Mediant, in the Treble Clef

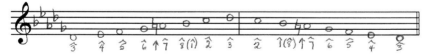

   $\hat{3}$  $\hat{4}$  $\hat{5}$  $\hat{6}$↑$\hat{7}$  $\hat{8}(\hat{1})$  $\hat{2}$  $\hat{3}$   $\hat{2}$  $\hat{1}(\hat{8})$↑$\hat{7}$  $\hat{6}$  $\hat{5}$  $\hat{4}$  $\hat{3}$

♫ **Note:** The Leading note is a semitone below the Tonic. In the Natural minor scale the $\hat{7}$ degree is a whole tone below the Tonic and is called the **SUBTONIC**.

   e) d minor natural, from Subtonic to Subtonic, in the Bass Clef

   $\hat{7}$  $\hat{8}(\hat{1})$  $\hat{2}$  $\hat{3}$  $\hat{4}$  $\hat{5}$  $\hat{6}$  $\hat{7}$   $\hat{6}$  $\hat{5}$  $\hat{4}$  $\hat{3}$  $\hat{2}$  $\hat{1}(\hat{8})$  $\hat{7}$

## MELODIC MINOR SCALES

When writing a **MELODIC MINOR SCALE**, the raised 6th and 7th notes are counted UP from the Tonic.

If the scale begins on the Submediant (6th degree), the raised 6th and 7th notes ( ↑6̂ ↑7̂ ) will be the first and second notes of the scale. The upper raised 6th degree is repeated - lowered at the beginning of the descending melodic minor scale. The 6th and 7th are lowered at the end of the scale.

e flat minor melodic, from Submediant to Submediant, using a Key Signature; with a center bar line.

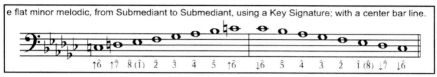

♫ **Note:** When using a center bar line, accidentals are not needed to lower the 6th and 7th notes. When NOT using a center bar line, accidentals WILL be needed in the descending scale.

1. Write the following melodic minor scales, ascending and descending, using a Key Signature. Use whole notes. Write the scale degree number below each note.

   a) c sharp minor melodic, from Submediant to Submediant, in the Alto Clef

   b) d minor melodic, from Submediant to Submediant, in the Treble Clef

♫ **Note:** When writing a melodic minor scale beginning on the LEADING NOTE, the raised 7th note is repeated - lowered in the descending melodic minor scale.

f minor melodic, from Leading note to Leading note, using a Key Signature; without a center bar line.

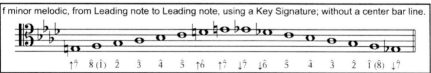

   c) a minor melodic, from Leading note to Leading note, in the Bass Clef

   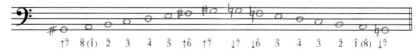

   d) g sharp minor melodic, from Leading note to Leading note, in the Alto Clef

21

## STYLE in PERFORMANCE

| Italian Term | Definition |
|---|---|
| *ad libitum, ad lib.* | at the liberty of the performer |
| *agitato* | agitated |
| *animato* | lively, animated |
| *brillante* | brilliant |
| *cantabile* | in a singing style |
| *con brio* | with vigor, spirit |
| *con espressione* | with expression |
| *con fuoco* | with fire |
| *con grazia* | with grace |
| *dolce* | sweet, gentle |
| *dolente* | sad |
| *espressivo, espress.* | expressive, with expression |

1. Write the definition for each of the following Italian terms.

| with grace | sad | with fire | sweet, gentle | agitated |
|---|---|---|---|---|
| *con grazia* | *dolente* | *con fuoco* | *dolce* | *agitato* |

| Italian Term | Definition |
|---|---|
| *giocoso* | humorous, jocose |
| *grandioso* | grand, grandiose |
| *grazioso* | graceful |
| *largamente* | broadly |
| *maestoso* | majestic |
| *mesto* | sad, mournful |
| *morendo* | dying, fading away |
| *scherzando* | playful |
| *semplice* | simple |
| *sonore* | sonorous |
| *sotto voce* | soft, subdued, under the breath |
| *spiritoso* | spirited |
| *tranquillo* | quiet, tranquil |
| *vivo* | lively |

2. Write the Italian term for each of the following definitions.

| grandioso | mesto | vivo | sonore | scherzando |
|---|---|---|---|---|
| grand, grandiose | sad, mournful | lively | sonorous | playful |

| giocoso | morendo | largamente | semplice | sotto voce |
|---|---|---|---|---|
| humorous, jocose | dying, fading away | broadly | simple | soft, subdued |

# Lesson 2                    Review Test

Write the Circle of Fifths on a blank piece of paper.  Use it as a reference while writing the review test.

**1.**  a)  Name the following intervals.

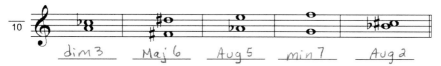

dim 3     Maj 6     Aug 5     min 7     Aug 2

b)  Invert the above intervals in the Bass Clef.  Use whole notes.  Name the inversions.

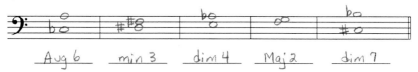

Aug 6     min 3     dim 4     Maj 2     dim 7

**2.**  a)  Name the **MAJOR KEY** for each of the following Key Signatures.
b)  Give the technical degree name for each note (Tonic, Supertonic, etc.).

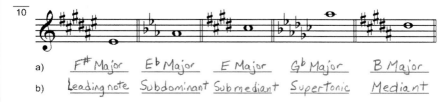

a)   F# Major    Eb Major    E Major    Gb Major    B Major

b)   Leading note   Subdominant   Submediant   Supertonic   Mediant

**3.**  For each of the following triads, name:
a)  the Root.
b)  the type/quality (Major or minor).
c)  the position (root, 1st inversion or 2nd inversion).

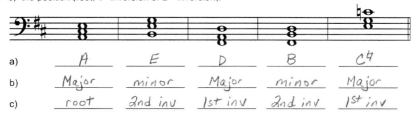

a)      A          E          D          B          C#

b)    Major     minor     Major     minor     Major

c)    root     2nd inv    1st inv    2nd inv    1st inv

**4.** Name the key of the following melody.
  a) Transpose the given melody **UP** a Major second in the Treble Clef. Use the correct Key Signature. Name the new key.
  10 b) Transpose the given melody **UP** a minor third in the Treble Clef. Use the correct Key Signature. Name the new key.

Key: _C Major_

a) Key: _D Major_

b) Key: _E♭ Major_

**5.** Write the Basic Beat and the pulse below each measure. Add rests below each bracket to complete the measure. Cross off the Basic Beat as each beat is completed.

24

**6.** Write the following scales, ascending and descending. Use the correct **KEY SIGNATURE**. Use whole notes.

10
   a) a sharp minor melodic, from Mediant to Mediant, in the Treble Clef
   b) e flat minor harmonic, from Submediant to Submediant, in the Alto Clef
   c) Tonic Major of e minor, from Subdominant to Subdominant, in the Tenor Clef
   d) c minor melodic, from Leading note to Leading note, in the Treble Clef
   e) relative minor, natural form, of D Major, from Tonic to Tonic, in the Bass Clef

Name the following scales as chromatic, octatonic, Major pentatonic, minor pentatonic or blues.

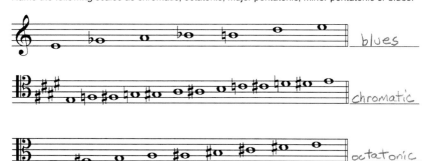

blues

chromatic

octatonic

25

**7.** a) Rewrite the following melody at the **SAME PITCH** in the **ALTO** Clef.

b) Rewrite the following melody at the **SAME PITCH** in the **BASS** Clef.

**8.** For each of the following cadences, name:
a) the key and chord symbols (V-I, iv-i, I-V, etc.).
b) the type (Perfect, Plagal or Imperfect).

a) c minor   iv   i     a) D Major   V   I     a) eb minor   i   V

b) Plagal            b) Perfect          b) Imperfect

9. Match each musical term with its English definition. (Not all definitions will be used.)

| Term | | Definition |
|---|---|---|
| langsam | _d_ | a) sad |
| ad libitum, ad lib. | _i_ | b) humorous, jocose |
| con fuoco | _k_ | c) agitated |
| giocoso | _b_ | d) slow; slowly |
| mässig | _h_ | e) with grace |
| agitato | _c_ | f) very |
| schnell | _j_ | g) playful |
| con grazia | _e_ | h) moderate; moderately |
| scherzando | _g_ | i) at the liberty of the performer |
| dolente | _a_ | j) fast |
| | | k) with fire |

10. Analyze the following piece of music by answering the questions below.

a) Add the correct Time Signature directly on the music.
b) Name the key of this piece. _G Major_
c) Name the interval at the letter **A**. _Perfect 4_
d) Name the interval at the letter **B**. _Major 3_
e) Give the technical degree name for the first note of the scale at the letter **C**. _Dominant_
f) Give the technical degree name for the first note of the scale at the letter **D**. _Leading note_
g) Name the type of rest at the letter **E**. _quarter rest_
h) Explain the sign at the letter **F**. _repeat sign-repeat the music_
i) How many measures are in this piece? _eight_
j) Locate and circle a whole tone in this piece. Label it as w.t.

27

# Lesson 3  Scales - Chromatic, Modes, Pentatonic, Blues, Octatonic, and Whole Tone

## CHROMATIC SCALES

A **HARMONIC** or a **MELODIC CHROMATIC SCALE** consists of 12 semitones (half steps) plus the upper Tonic for a total of 13 notes. No letter name may be written more than twice in a row. The scale must begin and end on the same letter name and cannot be changed enharmonically. It may be written with or without a Key Signature (using the Major Key Signature of the Tonic note). It may be written with or without a center bar line.

A **HARMONIC CHROMATIC** scale has a set form. It uses a single Tonic (I), Dominant (V) and upper Tonic (I) note ascending, and a single Dominant (V) and lower Tonic (I) note descending. All other notes are written twice. Double sharps or double flats may be necessary to write a note twice.

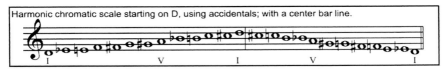

Harmonic chromatic scale starting on D, using accidentals; with a center bar line.

♫ **Note:** When writing the harmonic chromatic scale, write the notes in first, then add the accidentals.

1. Write the harmonic chromatic scale starting on G sharp, using accidentals. Use whole notes.

A **MELODIC CHROMATIC** scale does not have a set form. One standard notation for writing a melodic chromatic scale is to raise the semitones on the way up (ascending) and lower them on the way down (descending). There will be 5 single notes. All other notes are written twice.

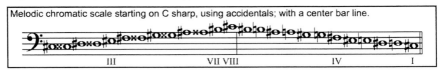

Melodic chromatic scale starting on C flat, using a Key Signature; with a center bar line.

Another standard notation is to write the melodic chromatic scale based on the Tonic Major scale, using a single note for the Mediant (III), Leading Note (VII) and upper Tonic (VIII) ascending, and a single Subdominant (IV) and lower Tonic (I) descending. All other notes are written twice.

Melodic chromatic scale starting on C sharp, using accidentals; with a center bar line.

2. Write the melodic chromatic scale starting on B, using a Key Signature. Use any standard notation.

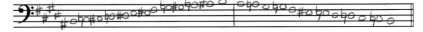

## MODES

A **MODE** is a 'SCALE' primarily used in Gregorian chants. Modes originated with the ancient Greeks. A Mode has the same pattern of tones and semitones as a Major Scale. Each mode begins on a different degree of the scale.

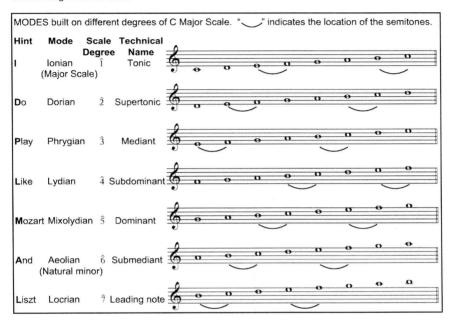

MODES built on different degrees of C Major Scale. "‿" indicates the location of the semitones.

| Hint | Mode | Scale Degree | Technical Name |
|------|------|--------------|----------------|
| I | Ionian (Major Scale) | 1̂ | Tonic |
| Do | Dorian | 2̂ | Supertonic |
| Play | Phrygian | 3̂ | Mediant |
| Like | Lydian | 4̂ | Subdominant |
| Mozart | Mixolydian | 5̂ | Dominant |
| And | Aeolian (Natural minor) | 6̂ | Submediant |
| Liszt | Locrian | 7̂ | Leading note |

♫ **Note:** Use the "**hint**" sentence to remember the modes: **I Do Play Like Mozart And Liszt.**

1. Write the "Hint", Mode and Technical Name for each of the following scale degrees.

| Hint | Mode | Scale Degree | Technical Name |
|------|------|--------------|----------------|
| I | Ionian | 1̂ | Tonic |
| Do | Dorian | 2̂ | Supertonic |
| Play | Phrygian | 3̂ | Mediant |
| Like | Lydian | 4̂ | Subdominant |
| Mozart | Mixolydian | 5̂ | Dominant |
| And | Aeolian | 6̂ | Submediant |
| Liszt | Locrian | 7̂ | Leading note |

## WRITING MODES

When **WRITING MODES**, use the "hint" sentence: **I** **D**o **P**lay **L**ike **M**ozart **A**nd **L**iszt. Write the letter name of the mode first, then count DOWN to determine the Tonic note of the Major Scale.

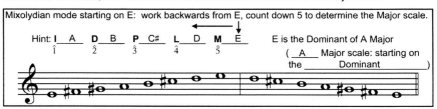

1. Write the note name of the mode. Work backwards to determine the Major key.
   Name the Major scale and the technical degree name of the first note of the scale.
   Write the following modes, ascending and descending, using accidentals. Use whole notes.

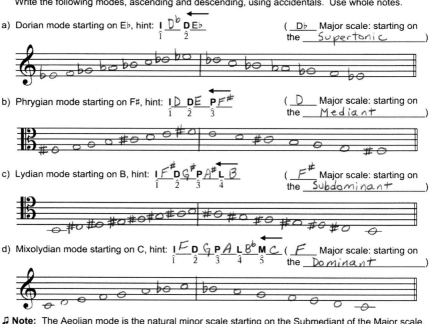

♪ **Note:** The Aeolian mode is the natural minor scale starting on the Submediant of the Major scale.

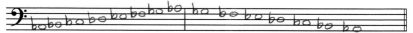

## IDENTIFYING MODES

When **IDENTIFYING MODES**, use the "hint" sentence: **I D**o **P**lay **L**ike **M**ozart **A**nd **L**iszt. Name the accidentals. Write the letter name of the Major key first, then count UP to determine the degree of the first note of the given mode.

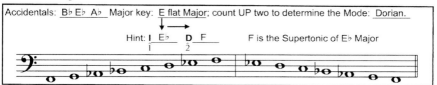

Accidentals: Bb Eb Ab  Major key: E flat Major; count UP two to determine the Mode: Dorian.

Hint: I Eb  D  F       F is the Supertonic of Eb Major

1. Name the accidentals. Write the letter name of the Major key first. Count UP to the degree of the first note of the given mode.
   Identify the modes as: Dorian, Phrygian, Lydian, Mixolydian or Aeolian.

a) Accidentals: F# C# G# D# A#      Major key: B Major  hint: I B D C# P D#
   Mode: Phrygian                                            1   2   3

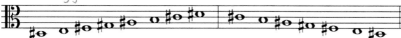

b) Accidentals: F# C# G# D#      Major key: E Major  hint: I E D F#
   Mode: Dorian                                           1   2

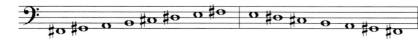

c) Accidentals: Bb Eb Ab Db Gb Cb   Major key: Gb Major  hint: I Gb D Ab P Bb L Cb M Db A Eb
   Mode: Aeolian                                          1   2    3    4    5   6

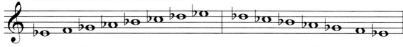

d) Accidentals: F#      Major key: G Major  hint: I G D A P B L C
   Mode: Lydian                                    1   2   3   4

e) Accidentals: F# C# G# D# A# E# B#   Major key: C# Major  hint: I C# D D# P E L F# M G#
   Mode: Mixolydian                                         1    2    3    4    5

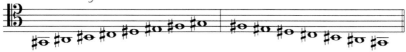

## MAJOR PENTATONIC, MINOR PENTATONIC and BLUES SCALES

A **PENTATONIC** scale (Penta means 5) consists of 5 notes plus the upper Tonic for a total of 6 notes.

A **Major pentatonic** scale is formed by taking a Major scale and omitting the 4th and 7th degrees.

A **minor pentatonic** scale is formed by taking the Major pentatonic scale beginning on the 6th degree.

♫ **Note:** A minor pentatonic scale is the natural minor scale, omitting the 2nd and 6th degrees.

A **BLUES** scale has 7 notes and may be formed by taking a minor pentatonic scale and **ADDING** the "**blue note**". The blue note is the raised 4th or lowered 5th degree (enharmonic equivalents).

A **blues** scale may also be formed by taking a Major scale and omitting the 2nd and 6th degrees and lowering the 3rd, 5th and 7th degrees one chromatic semitone. The 5th note is repeated; first lowered one semitone, then raised one semitone. The blue note may be written as its enharmonic equivalent.

1. Identify the following scales as Major pentatonic, minor pentatonic or blues scale.

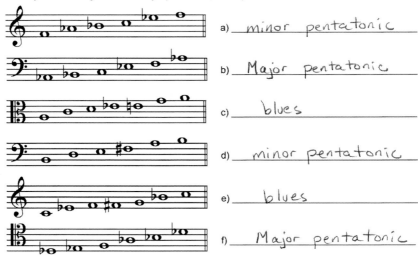

a) _minor pentatonic_

b) _Major pentatonic_

c) _blues_

d) _minor pentatonic_

e) _blues_

f) _Major pentatonic_

## OCTATONIC and WHOLE TONE SCALES

An **OCTATONIC** scale consists of 8 notes plus the upper Tonic for a total of 9 notes.

An **octatonic** scale is formed by alternating T (tone), ST (semitone), T (tone), ST (semitone), etc.
An **octatonic** scale is formed by alternating ST (semitone), T (tone), ST (semitone), T (tone), etc.

♫ **Note:** The Tonic note remains the same and may NOT be written as its enharmonic equivalent.

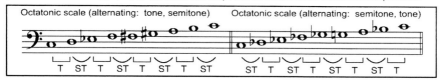

A **WHOLE TONE** scale consists of 6 consecutive whole tones. It has 6 different letter names plus the upper Tonic, for a total of 7 notes. A whole tone scale is written using sharps or flats (not both).

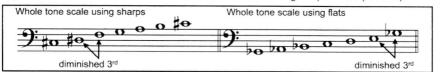

A **whole tone** scale, when using a keyboard, uses the group of two black keys or the group of three black keys. A whole tone scale omits one letter name and contains one interval of a diminished 3rd. The SAME notes are used ascending and descending. Do not change the Tonic note enharmonically.

1. Write the following scales, ascending and descending, using accidentals. Use whole notes.

   a) whole tone scale starting on G

   b) whole tone scale starting on A flat

   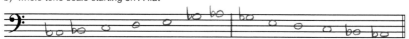

2. Identify the following scales as: Major pentatonic, minor pentatonic, blues, octatonic or whole tone.

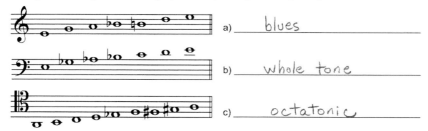

a) _____blues_____

b) _____whole tone_____

c) _____octatonic_____

**TEMPO and CHANGES in TEMPO**

**TEMPO and CHANGES in TEMPO** indicate the speed at which a piece is performed.

| Tempo | Definition |
|---|---|
| *adagio* | a slow tempo (slower than *andante,* but not as slow as *largo*) |
| *allegretto* | fairly fast (a little slower than *allegro*) |
| *allegro* | fast |
| *andante* | moderately slow; at a walking pace |
| *andantino* | a little faster than *andante* |
| *comodo* | at a comfortable, easy tempo |
| *con moto* | with movement |
| *grave* | slow and solemn |
| *larghetto* | not as slow as *largo* |
| *largo* | very slow |
| *lento* | slow |
| *moderato* | at a moderate tempo |
| *presto* | very fast |
| *prestissimo* | as fast as possible |
| *stringendo* | pressing, becoming faster |
| *vivace* | lively, brisk |

1. Write the definition for each of the following tempos.

con moto: <u>with movement</u>  grave: <u>slow and solemn</u>

larghetto: <u>not as slow as largo</u> andantino: <u>a little faster than andante</u>

| Changes in Tempo | Definition |
|---|---|
| *accelerando, accel.* | becoming quicker |
| *allargando, allarg.* | broadening, becoming slower |
| *a tempo* | return to the original tempo |
| *calando* | becoming slower and softer |
| *fermata,* ⌢ | pause; hold the note or rest longer than its written value |
| *l'istesso tempo* | the same tempo |
| *meno mosso* | less movement, slower |
| *più mosso* | more movement, quicker |
| *rallentando, rall.* | slowing down |
| *ritardando, rit.* | slowing down gradually |
| *ritenuto, riten.* | suddenly slower, held back |
| *rubato* | with some freedom of tempo to enhance musical expression |
| *Tempo primo, Tempo I* | return to the original tempo |

2. Write the definition for each of the following changes in tempos.

allargando: <u>broadening, becoming slower</u>  ritenuto: <u>suddenly slower, held back</u>

meno mosso: <u>less movement, slower</u>  calando: <u>becoming slower and softer</u>

## ARTICULATION and PEDAL

**ARTICULATION TERMS** and **SIGNS** indicate how a piece is performed.

| Articulation | Definition | Sign |
|---|---|---|
| *marcato,marc.* | marked or stressed | |
| *martellato* | strongly accented, hammered | |
| *accent* | a stressed note | |
| *pesante* | weighty, with emphasis | |
| *legato* | smooth | |
| *slur* | play the notes *legato* | |
| *leggiero* | light, nimble, quick | |
| *staccato* | detached | |
| *sostenuto* | sustained | |
| *tenuto* | held, sustained | |

♩ **Note:** An accent, slur, staccato or tenuto are written closest to the notehead and away from the stem. A fermata is always written above the staff.

For a single staff, dynamics are written **BELOW** the Treble Clef, Alto Clef and Tenor Clef, and **ABOVE** the Bass Clef. For a Grand Staff, they are written in between the Treble and Bass.

1. Copy the music below, adding all the articulation and dynamic markings.

| Pedal | Definition |
|---|---|
| *pedale, ped.* | pedal |
| *con pedale, con ped.* | with pedal |
| *tre corde* | three strings; release the left (piano) pedal |
| *una corda* | one string; depress the left (piano) pedal |
| ⌊_____⌋ , 𝄚 | pedal marking |

2. Write the definition for each of the following terms.

con pedale: <u>with pedal</u>  una corda: <u>one string, depress the left pedal</u>

pedale: <u>pedal</u>  tre corde: <u>three strings, release the left pedal</u>

# Lesson 3          Review Test

Total Score: ____
100

Write the Circle of Fifths on a blank piece of paper. Use it as a reference while writing the review test.

**1.** a) Name the following intervals.

dim 7      Aug 7      Maj 2      dim 3      Maj 3

b) Invert the above intervals in the Treble Clef. Use whole notes. Name the inversions.

Aug 2      dim 2      min 7      Aug 6      min 6

**2.** a) Name the **MINOR** key for each of the following Key Signatures.
b) Write the Dominant triad in root position for each harmonic minor key. Use whole notes.

a)    b♭ minor      f♯ minor    d minor      d♯ minor    g minor

**3.** For each of the following triads, name:
a) the Root.
b) the type/quality (Major or minor).
c) the position (root, 1st inversion or 2nd inversion).

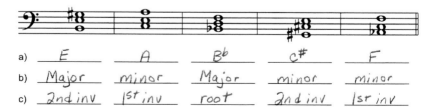

a)    E      A      B♭      c♯      F

b)    Major    minor    Major    minor    minor

c)    2nd inv   1st inv   root     2nd inv   1st inv

4. Name the key of the following melody. Transpose it **UP** a minor third in the Bass Clef. Use the correct Key Signature. Name the new key.

Key: ___F Major___

Key: ___Ab Major___

5. Write the Basic Beat and the pulse below each measure. Add rests below each bracket to complete the measure. Cross off the Basic Beat as each beat is completed.

Basic Beat: _____

Pulse: Sw wHww MwwMww Sww Mww MwwMww Sww Mww Mww Mww
S. w. M.+w. S. w.nM. w. S. w.nM.+w.

Basic Beat: _____

Pulse: Sww Mww Mwww S wnw M www Mww Sww Mww Mww
S. w. w. S. w.n w. S.+ w. w.

6. For each of the following cadences, name:
a) the key and chord symbols (V-I, iv-i, I-V, etc.).
b) the type (Perfect, Plagal or Imperfect).

a) a minor __iv__ __V__        a) B Major __IV__ __I__        a) f# minor __V__ __i__
b) Imperfect                   b) Plagal                      b) Perfect

**7.** Write the following scales, ascending and descending, using accidentals. Use whole notes.

___
10
    a) d sharp minor harmonic, from Mediant to Mediant, in the Treble Clef
    b) a flat minor melodic, from Submediant to Submediant, in the Alto Clef
    c) whole tone scale starting on F sharp in the Tenor Clef
    d) chromatic scale, using any standard notation, starting on G in the Bass Clef
    e) Lydian mode starting on A in the Treble Clef
    f) Dorian mode starting on C in the Bass Clef

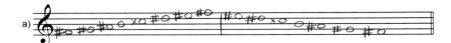

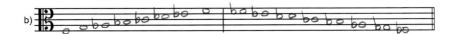

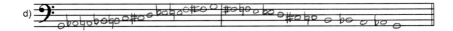

**8.** Identify the following scales as whole tone, blues, chromatic, octatonic, Major pentatonic or minor pentatonic.

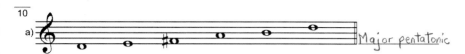

a) Major pentatonic

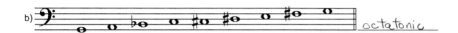

b) octatonic

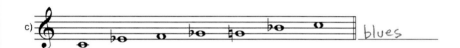

c) blues

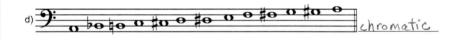

d) chromatic

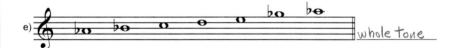

e) whole tone

f) minor pentatonic

g) blues

**9.** Match each musical term with its English definition. (Not all definitions will be used.)

| Term | | Definition |
|------|------|------------|
| grandioso | j | a) broadly |
| vivo | f | b) with vigor, spirit |
| largamente | a | c) soft, subdued, under the breath |
| mesto | h | d) dying, fading away |
| semplice | k | e) sonorous |
| sotto voce | c | f) lively |
| morendo | d | g) quiet, tranquil |
| sonore | e | h) sad, mournful |
| tranquillo | g | i) with expression |
| con brio | b | j) grand, grandiose |
| | | k) simple |

**10.** Analyze the following piece of music by answering the questions below.

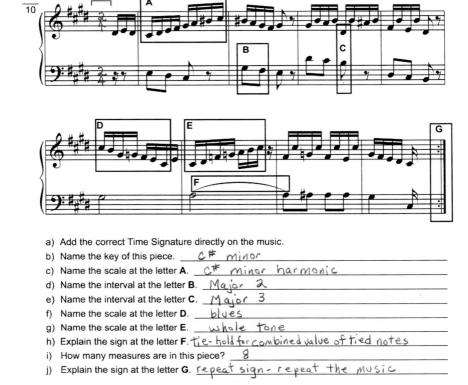

a) Add the correct Time Signature directly on the music.

b) Name the key of this piece. ___C# minor___

c) Name the scale at the letter **A**. ___C# minor harmonic___

d) Name the interval at the letter **B**. ___Major 2___

e) Name the interval at the letter **C**. ___Major 3___

f) Name the scale at the letter **D**. ___blues___

g) Name the scale at the letter **E**. ___whole tone___

h) Explain the sign at the letter **F**. ___tie- hold for combined value of tied notes___

i) How many measures are in this piece? ___8___

j) Explain the sign at the letter **G**. ___repeat sign- repeat the music___

# Lesson 4    Intervals - Simple, Compound and Inversions

**INTERVALS:** The type/quality of an interval changes when moving a chromatic semitone (half step).

Intervals 2, 3, 6, 7    **Diminished** <u>semitone</u> **minor** <u>semitone</u> **Major** <u>semitone</u> **Augmented**
dim                                                    min                                Maj                                Aug

Intervals 1, 4, 5, 8    **Diminished** <u>semitone</u> **Perfect** <u>semitone</u> **Augmented**
dim                                                    Per                                Aug

## Intervals BELOW a Given Note

To write an interval **BELOW** a given note, follow these steps:

Step 1:  Count down to determine the note that is the interval number below the given note. Write that note without an accidental.

Step 2:  Determine the type/quality of the interval (Augmented, Perfect, Major, minor or diminished) based upon the Major Key Signature of the bottom note.

Step 3:  Using accidentals (double sharp, sharp, flat or double flat), move one chromatic semitone (half step) at a time to adjust the bottom note until the correct interval is formed.

♫ **Note:** Do NOT change the given note. Determine the Major or Perfect interval below the given note first. Raise or lower the bottom note to form the correct interval. The bottom note may be a double flat or a double sharp.

---

**Harmonic interval** - Augmented 3 **BELOW** the given note D.

Down a 3rd from D is B. Key of B Major (F♯ C♯ G♯ D♯ A♯).
The interval of B to D is a min 3. (B to D♯ = Maj 3; B to D = min 3)
**Lower** the bottom note B to B♭. The interval of B♭ to D is a Maj 3.
**Lower** the bottom note B♭ to B♭♭. The interval of B♭♭ to D is an Augmented 3.

min 3    Maj 3    Aug 3

---

1. Write the following harmonic intervals below the given notes.

Aug 2        Aug 4        Maj 6        Per 5        Aug 7        min 3

---

**Melodic interval** - diminished 3 **BELOW** the given note E.

Down a 3rd from E is C. Key of C Major (no ♯s or ♭s).
The interval of C to E is a Maj 3.
**Raise** the bottom note C to C♯. C♯ to E is a min 3.
**Raise** the bottom note C♯ to C𝄪. The interval of C𝄪 to E is a diminished 3.

Maj 3    min 3    dim 3

---

2. Write the following melodic intervals below the given notes.

dim 3        Aug 6        dim 3        dim 5        Aug 7        Maj 2

41

## SIMPLE INTERVALS

A **SIMPLE INTERVAL** is NO LARGER than a Perfect octave. When writing intervals below a given note, always determine the Major or Perfect interval first. The bottom note determines the Major key.

♫ **Note:** Harmonic interval is written one note ABOVE the other, played together (at the same time). Melodic interval is written one note BESIDE the other, played one note after the other.

1. Write the following harmonic intervals below the given notes. Do not change the given note.

Maj 3    min 3    dim 3    Per 4    dim 4    Maj 6    min 6    dim 6

♫ **Note:** When writing a harmonic second below a given note, the lower note is written to the left. When there is **no room** for correct placement, it may be written to the right of the given note.

Maj 2    Aug 2    Per 4    Aug 4    Maj 6    Aug 6    Maj 7    Aug 7

2. Write the following melodic intervals below the given notes. Do not change the given note.

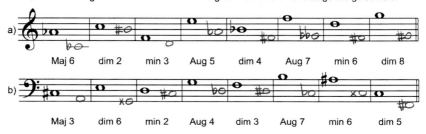

Maj 6    dim 2    min 3    Aug 5    dim 4    Aug 7    min 6    dim 8

b)

Maj 3    dim 6    min 2    Aug 4    dim 3    Aug 7    min 6    dim 5

If the bottom note is NOT a Major key on the Circle of Fifths, change the accidental to a Major key. Determine the interval based on the Major key.

Example: F♭♭ becomes F Major. Move the lower note, one semitone at a time, back to the original pitch to determine the given interval.

F♭♭ to A♭    F - A♭    F♭ - A♭    F♭♭ - A♭
             min 3     Maj 3      Aug 3

♫ **Note:** When both notes move up or down the same distance, the interval name remains the same. Example: Perfect 4: D to G, D♯ to G♯, D♭ to G♭, D♯ to G♯, D♭♭ to G♭♭

3. Name the following melodic intervals.

Aug 4    dim 7    Per 5    min 3    dim 2

## SIMPLE INTERVALS and INVERSIONS

An **INVERSION** of a **SIMPLE INTERVAL** is when the interval is turned upside down. A Simple interval and its inversion always equal 9. Example: A Major 3 becomes a minor 6 (3 + 6 = 9).

♫ **Note:** When inverting an interval: Major becomes minor, minor becomes Major, Augmented becomes diminished, diminished becomes Augmented and Perfect remains Perfect.

**Circle of Fifths**

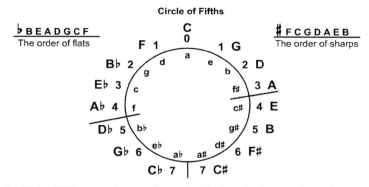

♭ B E A D G C F
The order of flats

♯ F C G D A E B
The order of sharps

1. Use the Circle of Fifths as a reference. For each of the following harmonic intervals:
   a) Name the interval. b) Invert the interval and name the inversion.

a) dim 5   Aug 7   dim 3   Per 5   dim 6   Maj 2   min 7   Aug 4

b) Aug 4   dim 2   Aug 6   Per 4   Aug 3   min 7   Maj 2   dim 5

a) min 3   dim 4   Maj 7   Per 8   dim 2   min 6   Aug 5   Aug 3

b) Maj 6   Aug 5   min 2   Per 1   Aug 7   Maj 3   dim 4   dim 6

43

## COMPOUND INTERVALS

A **COMPOUND INTERVAL** is LARGER than a Perfect octave. Identify a Compound interval as a Simple interval first by lowering the top note one octave or by raising the bottom note one octave.

♩ **Note:** The type/quality of a Simple interval is the **SAME** as the type/quality of a Compound interval. (Perfect, Major, minor, Augmented or diminished)

Naming a Compound (C) interval. Example: a dim 13 is also called a Compound dim 6 or C dim 6.

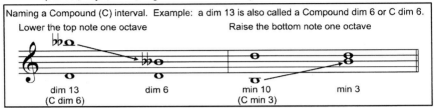

Lower the top note one octave        Raise the bottom note one octave

dim 13        dim 6        min 10        min 3
(C dim 6)                  (C min 3)

♩ **Note:** Name the Simple interval FIRST, then the Compound interval. They have the SAME quality. The Simple interval number **PLUS** "7" equals the Compound interval number.

1. Change the following Compound intervals into Simple intervals by lowering the top note one octave. Name the Simple interval first, then name the Compound interval.

a)   min 13    min 6    Maj 10    Maj 3    Per 11    Per 4    Aug 10    Aug 3

b)   min 9    min 2    Aug 12    Aug 5    dm 14    dim 7    Per 12    Per 5

♩ **Note:** The Compound interval number **MINUS** "7" equals the Simple interval number.

2. Change the following Compound intervals into Simple intervals by raising the bottom note one octave. Name the Simple interval first, then name the Compound interval.

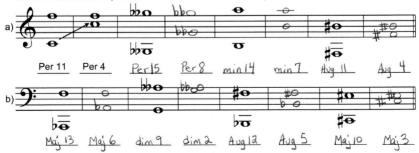

a)   Per 11    Per 4    Per 15    Per 8    min 14    min 7    Aug 11    Aug 4

b)   Maj 13    Maj 6    dim 9    dim 2    Aug 12    Aug 5    Maj 10    Maj 3

## COMPOUND INTERVALS and INVERSIONS

An **INVERSION** of a **COMPOUND INTERVAL** becomes a Simple interval. A Compound interval and its inversion always equal 16. Example: A Major 10 inverts to a minor 6 (10 + 6 = 16).

♪ **Note:** Inverting a Compound interval may be done by:
   a) lowering the top note TWO octaves.
   b) raising the bottom note TWO octaves.
   c) lowering the top note one octave AND raising the bottom note one octave.

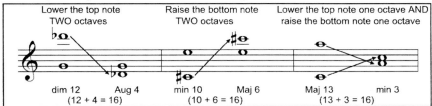

| Lower the top note TWO octaves | Raise the bottom note TWO octaves | Lower the top note one octave AND raise the bottom note one octave |
|---|---|---|
| dim 12     Aug 4 | min 10     Maj 6 | Maj 13     min 3 |
| (12 + 4 = 16) | (10 + 6 = 16) | (13 + 3 = 16) |

♪ **Note:** A Compound interval is the same quality as the Simple interval plus 7. (dim 4 + 7 = dim 11)

1. a) Rewrite the following Compound intervals as Simple intervals [in the square brackets].
      Name the Compound interval.
   b) Invert the Compound interval. (Use any method for inverting.) Name the inversion.

[dim 4] dim 11   Aug 5   [Maj 2] Maj 9   min 7   [Per 4] Per 11   Per 5   [min 6] min 13   Maj 3

♪ **Note:** An **Augmented 8** is a Compound interval (larger than an octave). When inverted, the Aug 8 becomes a dim 8, a Simple interval (smaller than an octave).

[min 3] min 10   Maj 6   [Aug 1] Aug 8   dim 8   [dim 4] dim 11   Aug 5   [dim 5] dim 12   Aug 4

A **Perfect 1 (unison)** is the smallest possible interval. If EITHER note of a Perfect 1 (unison) is raised or lowered a chromatic semitone, it becomes an Aug 1.

♪ **Note:** An interval is always named based upon the lowest note, therefore an interval of a first (unison) can NOT be diminished. It can only be Perfect or Augmented.

2. Name the following intervals.

Aug 1   Aug 1   Aug 1   Aug 1   dim 8   dim 8   Aug 8   Per 8   Aug 8

## ENHARMONIC EQUIVALENTS

An **ENHARMONIC EQUIVALENT** is the SAME PITCH written with a different note name. (Ab - G#)
All intervals have enharmonic equivalents. They have the same pitch or sound but are written using
different note names. The upper note, lower note or both notes may be changed enharmonically.

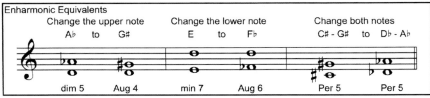

Enharmonic Equivalents

| Change the upper note | Change the lower note | Change both notes |
|---|---|---|
| Ab to G# | E to Fb | C# - G# to Db - Ab |
| dim 5   Aug 4 | min 7   Aug 6 | Per 5   Per 5 |

♫ **Note:** A dim 5 and an Aug 4 are enharmonic equivalent
intervals called a TRITONE. A tritone consists of
three whole tones (whole steps).

1. Name the following tritones. Write the enharmonic equivalent tritone. Name the new tritone.

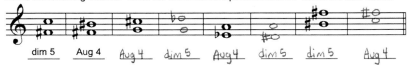

dim 5   Aug 4   Aug 4   dim 5   Aug 4   dim 5   dim 5   Aug 4

2. Name the following intervals. Change the upper notes enharmonically and rename the intervals.

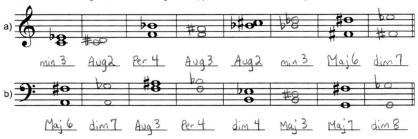

a)   min 3   Aug 2   Per 4   Aug 3   Aug 2   min 3   Maj 6   dim 7

b)   Maj 6   dim 7   Aug 3   Per 4   dim 4   Maj 3   Maj 7   dim 8

3. Name the following intervals. Change the lower notes enharmonically and rename the intervals.

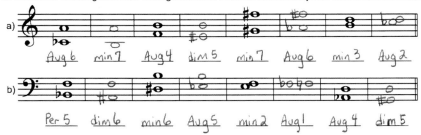

a)   Aug 6   min 7   Aug 4   dim 5   min 7   Aug 6   min 3   Aug 2

b)   Per 5   dim 6   min 6   Aug 5   min 2   Aug 1   Aug 4   dim 5

46

## ITALIAN TERMS

| Italian Term | Definition |
|---|---|
| *arco* | for stringed instruments: resume bowing after a *pizzicato* passage |
| *attacca* | proceed without a break |
| *con sordino* | with mute |
| *fine* | the end |
| *loco* | return to normal register |
| *ottava, $8^{va}$* | the interval of an octave |
| *pizzicato* | for stringed instruments: pluck the string instead of bowing |
| *primo, prima* | first; the upper part of a duet |
| *quindicesima alta, $15^{ma}$* | two octaves higher |
| *risoluto* | resolute |
| *secondo, seconda* | second; second or lower part of a duet |
| *simile* | continue in the same matter as has just been indicated |
| *tacet* | be silent |
| *tempo* | speed at which music is performed |
| *tutti* | a passage for the ensemble |
| *volta* | time (for example, *prima volta*, first time; *seconda volta*, second time) |
| *volti subito, v.s.* | turn the page quickly |

1. Write the term for each of the following definitions.

| tacet | fine | con sordino | volti subito, v.s. | risoluto |
|---|---|---|---|---|
| be silent | the end | with mute | turn the page quickly | resolute |

| | |
|---|---|
| *alla, all'* | in the manner of |
| *assai* | much, very much |
| *ben, bene* | well |
| *col, coll', colla, colle* | with |
| *con* | with |
| *e, ed* | and |
| *ma* | but |
| *meno* | less |
| *molto* | much, very |
| *non* | not |
| *non troppo* | not too much |
| *più* | more |
| *poco* | little |
| *poco a poco* | little by little |
| *quasi* | almost, as if |
| *sempre* | always, continuously |
| *senza* | without |
| *sopra* | above |
| *subito* | suddenly |
| *troppo* | too much |

2. Write the term for each of the following definitions.

| senza | non troppo | più | quasi | sempre |
|---|---|---|---|---|
| without | not too much | more | as if | always |

## ITALIAN TERMS and SIGNS, MEASURES and MAELZEL'S METRONOME

| Terms and Signs | Definitions |
|---|---|
| *D.C.* | *da capo*, from the beginning |
| *D.S.* | *dal segno*, from the sign 𝄋 |
| *D.C. al Fine* | repeat from the beginning and end at *Fine* (the end) |
| *M.D.* | *mano destra*, right hand |
| *M.S.* | *mano sinistra*, left hand |
| 𝄚 $8^{va}$- - - ┐ | *ottava*, $8^{va}$, play one octave above the written pitch |
| $8^{va}$- - - ┘ | *ottava*, $8^{va}$, play one octave below the written pitch |
| ♩‿♩ | *tie:* hold for the combined value of the tied notes |
| 𝄆 ‖ | *repeat signs*: repeat the music within the double bars |

**MEASURE** - unit of musical time. A single measure may be identified as "m." (example m. 4). More than one measure may be identified as "mm." (example mm. 1 - 4). One way of indicating measure numbers is by writing the number inside a small box above the top left of the measure.

♫ **Note:** A piece may begin and end with an incomplete measure. Together they equal one complete measure. The first COMPLETE measure is called measure number 1 (m. 1).

1. Write the measure number inside the square box above each measure.

**M.M.** means "Maelzel's Metronome" (named after Johann Maelzel). The metronome indicates sound of regular beats and thus an exact tempo (the speed at which the music is played). The M.M. is indicated by a small note (equal to one beat) followed by the number of beats per minute, identifying the tempo. Example: M.M. ♩ = 100 - 104 indicates 100 to 104 quarter note beats per minute.

♫ **Note:** The Tempo and metronome marking (M.M.) are BOTH written above the Time Signature.

2. Analyze the following piece of music by answering the questions below.

a) Explain the meaning of *Modéré*. <u>at a moderate tempo</u>

b) Explain the meaning at the letter **A**. <u>96-112 eighth note beats per minute</u>

c) Explain the meaning of the sign at the letter **B**. <u>play one octave higher than written</u>

d) When all signs are followed, how many measures are played? <u>4 (four)</u>

## ANALYSIS: IMITATION, SEQUENCE and INVERSION

**ANALYSIS** - relationship between the motive/phrase and **IMITATION, SEQUENCE** and **INVERSION**.

A **Motive** is the smallest unit of musical form that is used as a building block in music (2 - 7 notes, sometimes more). A **Phrase** is a musical unit of 4 (more or less) measures, ending with a cadence.

♫ **Note:** A musical idea may be a motive or larger, even a phase.

**Repetition** - the repeating of a musical idea by the **same** voice at the **same** pitch.

**Imitation** - the repetition of a musical idea (exact or varied) by **another** voice at the **same** pitch or at a **different** pitch. The imitation may be in the same clef or a different clef.

**Sequence** - the repetition of a musical idea by the **same** voice at a **higher** or **lower** pitch. Melodic sequence is in one voice. Harmonic sequence is in more than one voice.

**Inversion** - the musical idea is repeated "**upside-down**".
Melodic (interval) inversion occurs when interval directions of a single melodic line are reversed.
The inversion may not always be exact, as it is based on the melodic shape and chord structure.
Harmonic (voice) inversion occurs when one voice is transposed past another voice.

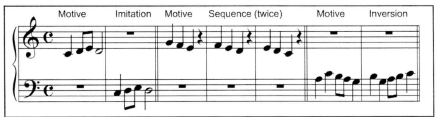

♫ **Note:** An "excerpt" is a passage taken from a piece of music.

1. For the excerpts below, give the term for the relationship between each motive and the measures at the following letters **A, B, C, D** and **E** as: repetition, imitation, sequence or inversion.

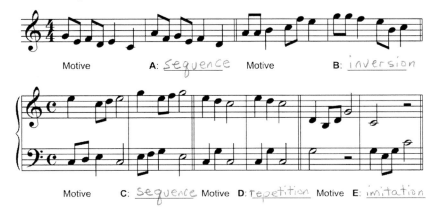

# Lesson 4        Review Test

Total Score: _____
100

Write the Circle of Fifths on a blank piece of paper. Use it as a reference while writing the review test.

**1.** a) Write the following harmonic intervals BELOW the given notes.

10

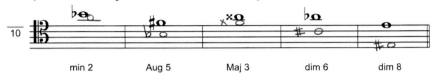

      min 2          Aug 5          Maj 3          dim 6          dim 8

b) Invert the above intervals in the Treble Clef. Use whole notes. Name the inversions.

     Maj 7        dim 4        min 6        Aug 3        Aug 1

**2.** For each of the following cadences, name:
     a) the key and chord symbols (V-I, iv-i, I-V, etc.).
     b) the type (Perfect, Plagal or Imperfect).

10

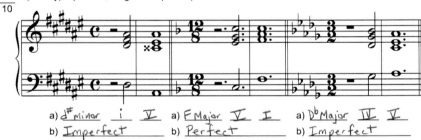

a) d# minor   i   V    a) F Major   V   I    a) Db Major   IV   V
b) Imperfect         b) Perfect         b) Imperfect

**3.** Write the following solid triads in the Bass Clef. Use whole notes. Use the correct **KEY SIGNATURE** for each.
     a) the **SUPERTONIC** triad of E Major in root position
10 b) the **DOMINANT** triad of d minor harmonic in second inversion
     c) the **SUBMEDIANT** triad of A flat Major in root position
     d) the **TONIC** triad of c minor harmonic in first inversion
     e) the **SUBDOMINANT** triad of F sharp Major in second inversion

     a)          b)          c)          d)          e)

**4.** Name the key of the following melody.

    a) Transpose the given melody **UP** a Perfect fifth in the Treble Clef. Use the correct Key Signature. Name the new key.

10  b) Transpose the given melody **UP** a minor third in the Treble Clef. Use the correct Key Signature. Name the new key.

Key: G Major

a) Key: D Major

b) Key: B♭ Major

**5.** Write the Basic Beat and the pulse below each measure. Add rests below each bracket to complete the measure. Cross off the Basic Beat as each beat is completed.

10

51

**6.** a) Name the following intervals. Change the **UPPER** notes **ENHARMONICALLY** and rename the intervals.

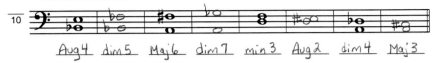

Aug4   dim5   Maj6   dim7   min3   Aug2   dim4   Maj3

b) Name the following intervals. Change the **LOWER** notes **ENHARMONICALLY** and rename the intervals.

Aug6   min7   min7   Aug6   Maj6   dim7   Aug3   Per4

**7.** Name the following **COMPOUND** intervals.   Invert the intervals and name the inversions.

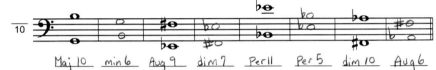

Maj10   min6   Aug9   dim7   Per11   Per5   dim10   Aug6

**8.** Write the following scales, ascending and descending.  Use the correct Key Signature. Use whole notes.
   a) b minor melodic, from Submediant to Submediant, in the Treble Clef
   b) e flat minor harmonic, from Supertonic to Supertonic, in the Alto Clef
   c) Tonic Major of a minor, from Subdominant to Subdominant, in the Tenor Clef
   d) Phrygian mode starting on C sharp in the Treble Clef
   e) Mixolydian mode starting on F in the Bass Clef

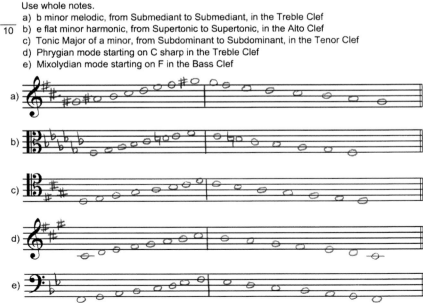

52

9.  Match each musical term with its English definition. (Not all definitions will be used.)

**Term**

10  quindicesima alta, 15^ma    _f_

risoluto    _j_

pizzicato    _a_

arco    _k_

attacca    _g_

con sordino    _i_

primo, prima    _c_

simile    _e_

tacet    _b_

tutti    _d_

**Definition**

a) stringed instruments: pluck the string instead of bowing

b) be silent

c) first; the upper part of a duet

d) a passage for the ensemble

e) continue in the same matter as just indicated

f) two octaves higher

g) proceed without a break

h) turn the page quickly

i) with mute

j) resolute

k) for stringed instruments: resume bowing after a pizzicato passage

10. Analyze the following excerpt by answering the questions below.

# Invention No. 4

J. S. Bach
(1685 - 1750)

10   **Allegro** M.M. ♪ = 60 - 72

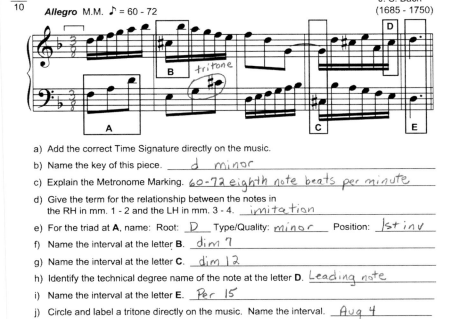

a) Add the correct Time Signature directly on the music.

b) Name the key of this piece. _d minor_

c) Explain the Metronome Marking. _60-72 eighth note beats per minute_

d) Give the term for the relationship between the notes in the RH in mm. 1 - 2 and the LH in mm. 3 - 4. _imitation_

e) For the triad at **A**, name: Root: _D_ Type/Quality: _minor_ Position: _1st inv_

f) Name the interval at the letter **B**. _dim 7_

g) Name the interval at the letter **C**. _dim 12_

h) Identify the technical degree name of the note at the letter **D**. _Leading note_

i) Name the interval at the letter **E**. _Per 15_

j) Circle and label a tritone directly on the music. Name the interval. _Aug 4_

# Lesson 5

## Triads and Inversions
## Major, Minor, Augmented and Diminished

A **TRIAD** is a three note chord. The lowest note of a root position triad (all lines or all spaces) is called the **Root**. A root position triad consists of a third and a fifth above the Root. The type/quality of the triad (Major, minor, Augmented or diminished) is determined by the type/quality of the intervals above the Root (Major or minor 3; Perfect, Augmented or diminished 5).

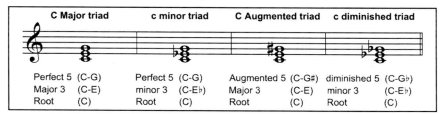

| C Major triad | c minor triad | C Augmented triad | c diminished triad |
|---|---|---|---|
| Perfect 5 (C-G) | Perfect 5 (C-G) | Augmented 5 (C-G#) | diminished 5 (C-Gb) |
| Major 3 (C-E) | minor 3 (C-Eb) | Major 3 (C-E) | minor 3 (C-Eb) |
| Root (C) | Root (C) | Root (C) | Root (C) |

♫ **Note:** **Major** triad: Root, Maj 3, Per 5      **minor** triad: Root, min 3, Per 5
**Augmented** triad: Root, Maj 3, Aug 5      **diminished** triad: Root, min 3, dim 5

1. Copy the chart to determine the type/quality of a Major, minor, Augmented or diminished triad.

Maj 3 + Per 5  = **Major triad**        <u>Maj</u> 3 + <u>Per</u> 5 = **Major triad**

min 3 + Per 5  = **minor triad**        <u>min</u> 3 + <u>Per</u> 5 = **minor triad**

Maj 3 + Aug 5  = **Augmented triad**        <u>Maj</u> 3 + <u>Aug</u> 5 = **Augmented triad**

min 3 + dim 5  = **diminished triad**        <u>min</u> 3 + <u>dim</u> 5 = **diminished triad**

2. a) Name the type/quality of the interval of a fifth above the Root as Per, Aug or dim.
   b) Name the type/quality of the interval of a third above the Root as Maj or min.
   c) Name the type/quality of the triad as Major, minor, Augmented or diminished.

a) Fifth: <u>Aug</u> 5   <u>Aug</u> 5   <u>Per</u> 5   <u>Per</u> 5   <u>Aug</u> 5   <u>dim</u> 5

b) Third: <u>Maj</u> 3   <u>Maj</u> 3   <u>min</u> 3   <u>Maj</u> 3   <u>Maj</u> 3   <u>min</u> 3

c) Triad: <u>Augmented</u>   <u>Augmented</u>   <u>minor</u>   <u>Major</u>   <u>Augmented</u>   <u>diminished</u>

a) Fifth: <u>dim</u> 5   <u>Per</u> 5   <u>dim</u> 5   <u>Aug</u> 5   <u>Per</u> 5   <u>Aug</u> 5

b) Third: <u>min</u> 3   <u>Maj</u> 3   <u>min</u> 3   <u>Maj</u> 3   <u>min</u> 3   <u>Maj</u> 3

c) Triad: <u>diminished</u>   <u>Major</u>   <u>diminished</u>   <u>Augmented</u>   <u>minor</u>   <u>Augmented</u>

## TRIADS on SCALE DEGREES

**TRIADS** may be built on any scale degree of a Major or minor scale. **Functional Chord Symbols** are Roman Numerals that are used to identify the type/quality and scale degree of a triad (chord).

♫ **Note:** **Major (Maj)** triads: Upper case Roman Numerals.
   **Minor (min)** triads: lower case Roman Numerals.
   **Augmented (Aug)** triads: Upper case Roman Numerals and an ✕ or + sign.
   **Diminished (dim)** triads: lower case Roman Numerals and a ° degree sign.

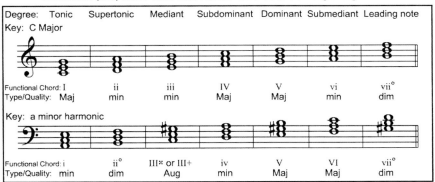

Degree: Tonic   Supertonic   Mediant   Subdominant   Dominant   Submediant   Leading note
Key: C Major

| Functional Chord: | I | ii | iii | IV | V | vi | vii° |
| Type/Quality: | Maj | min | min | Maj | Maj | min | dim |

Key: a minor harmonic

| Functional Chord: | i | ii° | III✕ or III+ | iv | V | VI | vii° |
| Type/Quality: | min | dim | Aug | min | Maj | Maj | dim |

♫ **Note:** Triads built on the Mediant, Dominant and Leading note of the harmonic minor scale always contain the raised 7th note.

1. Write a solid root position triad above each note of the g minor harmonic scale. Use whole notes.
   Name the type/quality as Major (Maj), minor (min), Augmented (Aug) or diminished (dim).

|  | i | ii° | III✕ or III+ | iv | V | VI | vii° |
| Type/Quality: | min | dim | Aug | min | Maj | Maj | dim |

2. Write the following solid root position triads using accidentals, in the Bass Clef. Use whole notes.
   Name the type/quality as Major, minor, Augmented or diminished.

   a) the **SUPERTONIC** triad (ii) of E flat Major
   b) the **LEADING NOTE** triad (vii°) of d sharp minor harmonic
   c) the **DOMINANT** triad (V) of f minor harmonic
   d) the **MEDIANT** triad (III✕ or III+) of b minor harmonic
   e) the **SUBMEDIANT** triad (VI) of a flat minor harmonic

| a) | b) | c) | d) | e) |
| Type/Quality: min | dim | Maj | Aug | Maj |

## TRIADS IN CLOSE POSITION

**TRIADS** in **CLOSE POSITION** are written as close together as possible. NO interval is larger than a sixth. **Figured bass** (chord position) numbers are used to indicate the position of a triad. Each number represents the interval distance ABOVE the lowest note of the triad.

♫ **Note:** In **CLOSE POSITION**, the **position** (root, 1st inv or 2nd inv) of a triad is determined by the lowest note. The lowest note of a **root position triad** names the Root of the triad.

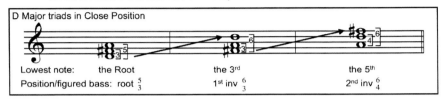

D Major triads in Close Position

Lowest note: the Root — the 3rd — the 5th

Position/figured bass: root $\frac{5}{3}$ — 1st inv $\frac{6}{3}$ — 2nd inv $\frac{6}{4}$

1. For each of the following triads, name:
   a) the Root. Write the triad in root position in [square brackets]. (Lowest note names the Root.)
   b) the type/quality (Major, minor, Augmented or diminished).
   c) the position and figured bass (root $\frac{5}{3}$, 1st inv $\frac{6}{3}$ or 2nd inv $\frac{6}{4}$).

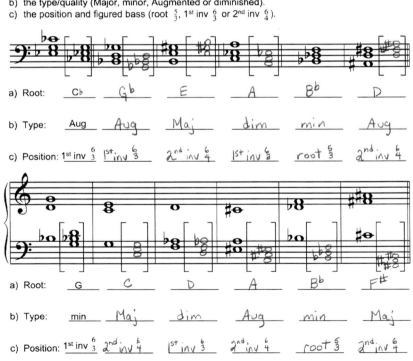

a) Root:   C♭    G♭    E    A    B♭    D

b) Type:   Aug    Aug    Maj    dim    min    Aug

c) Position: 1st inv $\frac{6}{3}$  1st inv $\frac{6}{3}$  2nd inv $\frac{6}{4}$  1st inv $\frac{6}{3}$  root $\frac{5}{3}$  2nd inv $\frac{6}{4}$

a) Root:   G    C    D    A    B♭    F♯

b) Type:   min    Maj    dim    Aug    min    Maj

c) Position: 1st inv $\frac{6}{3}$  2nd inv $\frac{6}{4}$  1st inv $\frac{6}{3}$  2nd inv $\frac{6}{4}$  root $\frac{5}{3}$  2nd inv $\frac{6}{4}$

## TRIADS in OPEN POSITION

**TRIADS** in **OPEN POSITION** are written on one staff or on the Grand Staff. The triad is spread out over more than an octave. When one of the notes (usually the root) is doubled, the triad is in four note form. Open position and closed position triads use the same chord positions and figured bass.

♫ **Note:** In **OPEN POSITION**, the position of a triad is determined by the lowest note. The other notes may be written in ANY order above the lowest note.

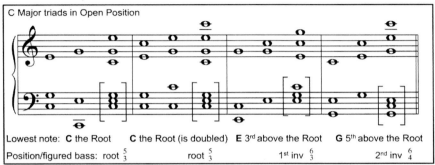

| Lowest note: | C the Root | C the Root (is doubled) | E 3rd above the Root | G 5th above the Root |
|---|---|---|---|---|
| Position/figured bass: | root $\frac{5}{3}$ | root $\frac{5}{3}$ | 1st inv $\frac{6}{3}$ | 2nd inv $\frac{6}{4}$ |

1. Fill in the blanks:
   a) When in root position (Close or Open position), the lowest note names the __Root__.

   b) The position of a triad (Close or Open position) is determined by the __lowest__ note.

   c) Write the figured bass for: root position - $\frac{5}{3}$ ; 1st inv - $\frac{6}{3}$ ; 2nd inv - $\frac{6}{4}$ .

2. For each of the following triads, name:
   a) the Root. Write the triad in root position in [square brackets]. (Lowest note names the Root.)
   b) the type/quality (Major, minor, Augmented or diminished).
   c) the position and figured bass (root $\frac{5}{3}$, 1st inv $\frac{6}{3}$ or 2nd inv $\frac{6}{4}$).

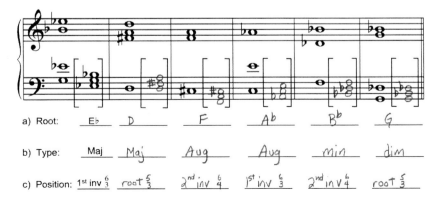

a) Root:    Eb    D     F     Ab     Bb     G

b) Type:    Maj    Maj    Aug    Aug    min    dim

c) Position: 1st inv $\frac{6}{3}$   root $\frac{5}{3}$   2nd inv $\frac{6}{4}$   1st inv $\frac{6}{3}$   2nd inv $\frac{6}{4}$   root $\frac{5}{3}$

**WRITING MAJOR, MINOR, AUGMENTED and DIMINISHED TRIADS and INVERSIONS**

When writing **MAJOR, MINOR, AUGMENTED** or **DIMINISHED** triads, always start with root position. Determine the intervals above the Root to create the triad. The third and fifth above the Root determine the type/quality of the triad. Then write the triad in the inverted position.

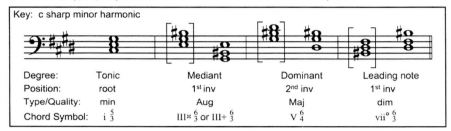

Key: c sharp minor harmonic

| Degree: | Tonic | Mediant | Dominant | Leading note |
|---|---|---|---|---|
| Position: | root | 1st inv | 2nd inv | 1st inv |
| Type/Quality: | min | Aug | Maj | dim |
| Chord Symbol: | i $\frac{5}{3}$ | III⨯ $\frac{6}{3}$ or III+ $\frac{6}{3}$ | V $\frac{6}{4}$ | vii° $\frac{6}{3}$ |

♫ **Note:** The **CHORD SYMBOL** will show the **Functional Chord Symbol** (Roman Numeral) and the **Figured Bass** (position numbers).

1.  Write the following triads in close position using the correct Key Signature. Use whole notes. Name the type/quality. Write the chord symbol for each triad.

    a) the **MEDIANT** triad of g minor harmonic in second inversion
    b) the **LEADING NOTE** triad of b minor harmonic in first inversion
    c) the **DOMINANT** triad of A flat Major in second inversion
    d) the **SUPERTONIC** triad of B Major in root position
    e) the **SUBMEDIANT** triad of e minor harmonic in first inversion

| | a) | b) | c) | d) | e) |
|---|---|---|---|---|---|
| Type/Quality: | Aug | dim | Maj | min | Maj |
| Chord Symbol: | III+ $\frac{6}{4}$ | vii° $\frac{6}{3}$ | V $\frac{6}{4}$ | ii $\frac{5}{3}$ | VI $\frac{6}{3}$ |

2.  Write the following triads in close position using accidentals. Use whole notes. Name the type/quality. Write the chord symbol for each triad.

    a) the **TONIC** triad of a flat minor harmonic in second inversion
    b) the **SUBDOMINANT** triad of f sharp minor harmonic in root position
    c) the **MEDIANT** triad of G flat Major in first inversion
    d) the **DOMINANT** triad of c sharp minor harmonic in first inversion
    e) the **LEADING NOTE** triad of D flat Major in root position

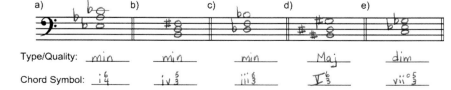

| | a) | b) | c) | d) | e) |
|---|---|---|---|---|---|
| Type/Quality: | min | min | min | Maj | dim |
| Chord Symbol: | i $\frac{6}{4}$ | iv $\frac{5}{3}$ | iii $\frac{6}{3}$ | V $\frac{6}{3}$ | vii° $\frac{5}{3}$ |

## IDENTIFYING a SCALE WHICH CONTAINS a GROUP of TRIADS

When **IDENTIFYING** a **SCALE WHICH CONTAINS** a **GROUP** of **TRIADS**, write the accidentals in the order of the Key Signature. If the triads are written using accidentals in correct Key Signature order, the scale will be Major and its relative natural minor. If the accidentals are not in correct Key Signature order, a triad will contain the raised 7th note, and the scale will be the harmonic minor.

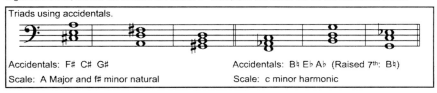

Accidentals: F♯ C♯ G♯

Scale: A Major and f♯ minor natural

Accidentals: B♭ E♭ A♭ (Raised 7th: B♮)

Scale: c minor harmonic

1. For each of the triads, name: a) the accidentals. b) the scale which contains all of the triads.

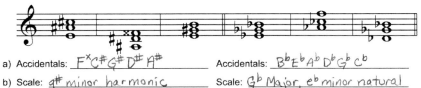

a) Accidentals: F<sup>x</sup>C♯G♯D♯A♯   Accidentals: B♭E♭A♭D♭G♭C♭

b) Scale: g♯ minor harmonic   Scale: G♭ Major, e♭ minor natural

♫ **Note:** If a Key Signature is used and no accidental appears with a triad, the scale which contains a group of triads (Major, minor or diminished) belongs to a Major scale and its relative natural minor scale. If an accidental (raised 7th note) is used, the scale which contains a group of triads (Major, minor, Augmented or diminished) belongs to a harmonic minor scale.

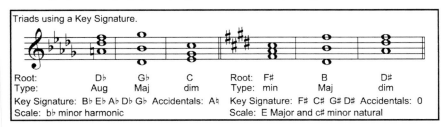

Triads using a Key Signature.

| | Root: | D♭ | G♭ | C | Root: | F♯ | B | D♯ |
| | Type: | Aug | Maj | dim | Type: | min | Maj | dim |

Key Signature: B♭ E♭ A♭ D♭ G♭ Accidentals: A♮   Key Signature: F♯ C♯ G♯ D♯ Accidentals: 0

Scale: b♭ minor harmonic   Scale: E Major and c♯ minor natural

2. For each of the triads, name: a) the Root. b) the type. c) the Key Signature and any accidentals. d) the scale which contains all of the triads.

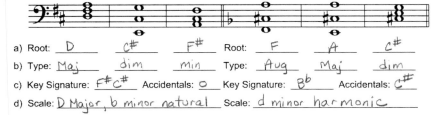

a) Root: D    C♯    F♯    Root: F    A    C♯

b) Type: Maj    dim    min    Type: Aug    Maj    dim

c) Key Signature: F♯C♯    Accidentals: 0    Key Signature: B♭    Accidentals: C♯

d) Scale: D Major, b minor natural    Scale: d minor harmonic

59

# Lesson 5      Review Test

Total Score: _____
100

Write the Circle of Fifths on a blank piece of paper. Use it as a reference when doing the review test.

**1.** a) Name the following intervals.

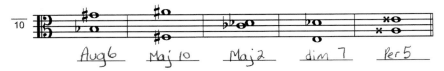

10

Aug 6     Maj 10     Maj 2     dim 7     Per 5

b) Invert the above intervals in the Bass Clef. Use whole notes. Name the inversions.

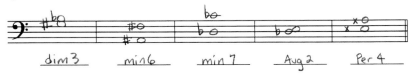

dim 3     min 6     min 7     Aug 2     Per 4

**2.** Write the following triads in the Bass Clef, using the correct **KEY SIGNATURE** for each. Use whole notes.

a) the **LEADING NOTE** triad of f sharp minor harmonic in first inversion

10 b) the **MEDIANT** triad of c minor harmonic in second inversion

c) the **SUBDOMINANT** triad of A Major in first inversion

d) the **SUPERTONIC** triad of D flat Major in root position

e) the **SUBMEDIANT** triad of e minor harmonic in second inversion

a)          b)          c)          d)          e)

**3.** For each of the following triads, name:

a) the Root.

b) the type/quality (Major, minor, Augmented or diminished).

10 c) the position (root, 1st inversion or 2nd inversion).

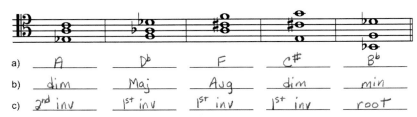

a)    A       Db       F       C#       Bb

b)    dim      Maj      Aug      dim      min

c)    2nd inv    1st inv    1st inv    1st inv    root

**4.** Name the key of the following melody.

    a) Transpose the given melody **UP** a minor sixth in the Alto Clef. Use the correct Key Signature.
       Name the new key.

10  b) Rewrite the given melody at the **SAME PITCH** in the Tenor Clef. Use the correct Key Signature.

Key: C Major

a)

Key: A♭ Major

b)

**5.** Write the Basic Beat and the pulse below each measure. Add rests below each bracket to complete the measure. Cross off the Basic Beat as each beat is completed.

10

61

**6.** Write the following scales, ascending and descending, in the clefs indicated.  Use the correct **KEY SIGNATURE**.  Use whole notes.

_10_
    a) g sharp minor melodic, from leading note to leading note, in the Treble Clef
    b) Dorian mode starting on F in the Alto Clef
    c) E Major, from supertonic to supertonic, in the Tenor Clef
    d) chromatic scale starting on B flat in the Bass Clef
    e) Mixolydian mode starting on G sharp in the Treble Clef

a)

b)

c)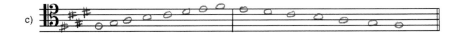

d)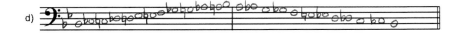

e)

**7.** Match each musical term with its English definition.  (Not all definitions will be used.)

_10_

| Term | | Definition |
|---|---|---|
| poco a poco | d | a) broadening, becoming slower |
| allargando | a | b) more movement, quicker |
| sforzando, *sf*, *sfz* | k | c) pressing, becoming faster |
| leggiero | g | d) little by little |
| più mosso | b | e) right hand |
| animato | i | f) graceful |
| grazioso | f | g) light, nimble, quick |
| stringendo | c | h) detached |
| mano destra | e | i) lively, animated |
| staccato | h | j) left hand |
| | | k) a sudden strong accent of a single note or chord |

**8.** Name the following scales as Major, harmonic minor, melodic minor, natural minor, chromatic, whole tone, octatonic, blues, Major pentatonic or minor pentatonic.

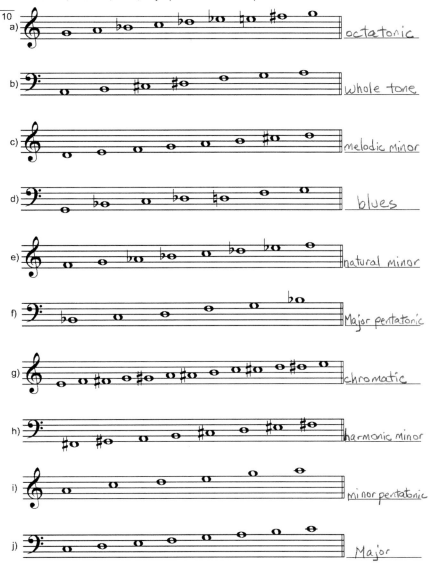

a) octatonic

b) whole tone

c) melodic minor

d) blues

e) natural minor

f) Major pentatonic

g) chromatic

h) harmonic minor

i) minor pentatonic

j) Major

**9.** For each of the following cadences, name:
a) the key and chord symbols (V-I, iv-i, I-V, etc.).
b) the type (Perfect, Plagal or Imperfect).

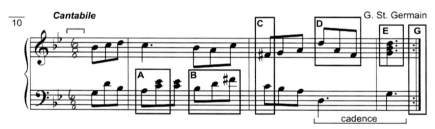

a) e minor    iv    i       a) Bb Major    IV    V       a) a# minor    i    V
b) Plagal                   b) Imperfect                 b) Imperfect

**10.** Analyze the following piece of music by answering the questions below.

**Cantabile**                                                          G. St. Germain

cadence

a) Add the correct Time Signature directly on the music.

b) Name the key of this piece. _g minor_

c) For the triad at **A**, name: Root: _A_ Type/Quality: _dim_ Position: _root_

d) For the triad at **B**, name: Root: _Bb_ Type/Quality: _Aug_ Position: _root_

e) Name the interval at the letter **C**. _Aug 4_

f) For the triad at **D**, name: Root: _D_ Type/Quality: _Major_ Position: _1st inv_

g) For the triad at **E**, name: Root: _G_ Type/Quality: _minor_ Position: _root_

h) When adding the Bass notes to the triads at the letter **D** and **E**,
what cadence is formed? (Perfect, Plagal or Imperfect) _Perfect_

i) Name the scale that contains all the triads at the letters **A, B, D, E.** _g minor harmonic_

j) Explain the sign at the letter **G**. _repeat sign - repeat the music_

# Lesson 6   Dominant Seventh and Diminished Seventh Chords

The **DOMINANT SEVENTH** chord is a four note chord that is built on the fifth degree of a scale.  It consists of a Root, Major 3, Perfect 5 and a minor 7.  The symbol for the **Dominant 7th** chord is V7. The Roman Numeral V indicates the fifth degree above the Tonic.  The number 7 after the Roman Numeral (V7) indicates the Dominant (Major) triad with an interval of a minor 7th above the Root.

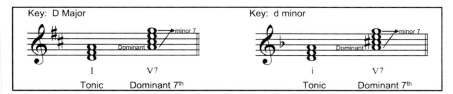

♫ **Note:** Tonic Major and minor keys have the SAME Dominant 7th chord.  The Dominant 7th chord of a minor key always contains the raised 7th note of the harmonic minor scale.

1. For each of the following keys, write the Dominant seventh chord in root position.  Use accidentals.  Use whole notes.

  G Major    g minor    Bb Major    bb minor    E Major    e minor    D Major    d minor

Dominant 7th chords written using a Key Signature belong to either the Major or relative minor key. (The minor key contains the raised 7th note.)  To identify the Major or minor key of a Dominant chord, count DOWN a Perfect fifth from the bottom note (the Root) of the Dominant 7th chord.

2. Name the key (Major or minor) to which the following Dominant seventh chords belong.

  <u>F Major</u>    <u>f minor</u>    <u>G Major</u>    <u>g minor</u>    <u>C Major</u>    <u>c minor</u>    <u>E Major</u>    <u>e minor</u>

Dominant seventh chords written using accidentals belong to BOTH the Major and Tonic minor keys.

3. Name the TWO keys (Major and Tonic minor) to which the following Dominant 7th chords belong.

  <u>D Maj / d min</u>    <u>Ab Maj / ab min</u>    <u>B Maj / b min</u>    <u>C Maj / c min</u>    <u>G Maj / g min</u>

## DOMINANT 7th CHORDS in CLOSE POSITION

**DOMINANT 7th chords in CLOSE POSITION** are written as close together as possible. NO interval is larger than a seventh. **Figured Bass** (chord position) numbers are used to indicate the position of a chord. Each number represents the interval distance ABOVE the lowest note of the chord. There are **3 inversions** of the Dominant 7th chord. The position of a chord is determined by the lowest note.

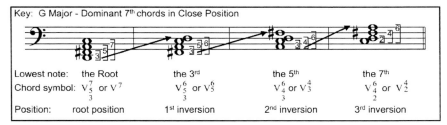

| | | | | |
|---|---|---|---|---|
| Lowest note: | the Root | the 3rd | the 5th | the 7th |
| Chord symbol: | $V_5^7$ or $V^7$ | $V_5^6$ or $V_5^6$ | $V_4^6$ or $V_3^4$ | $V_4^6$ or $V_2^4$ |
| Position: | root position | 1st inversion | 2nd inversion | 3rd inversion |

1. For each of the following Dominant seventh chords, name:
   a) the Root. Write the chord in root position in [square brackets]. (Lowest note names the Root.)
   b) the keys to which it belongs (Major and Tonic minor).
   c) the position (root position, 1st inv, 2nd inv or 3rd inv); the chord symbol ( $V^7$, $V_5^6$, $V_3^4$ or $V_2^4$ ).

| | | | | | | |
|---|---|---|---|---|---|---|
| a) Root: | G | D | A | B♭ | E | C |
| b) Maj key: | C Maj | G Maj | D Maj | E♭ Maj | A Maj | F Maj |
| min key: | c min | g min | d min | e♭ min | a min | f min |
| c) Position: | 1st inv | 2nd inv | 3rd inv | 1st inv | 3rd inv | 2nd inv |
| Symbol: | $V_5^6$ | $V_3^4$ | $V_2^4$ | $V_5^6$ | $V_2^4$ | $V_3^4$ |

2. Write the following Dominant seventh chords in the Bass Clef. Use the correct Key Signature. Use whole notes. Write the chord symbol for each.
   a) the Dominant seventh chord of e minor harmonic in 2nd inversion
   b) the Dominant seventh chord of b minor harmonic in 1st inversion
   c) the Dominant seventh chord of D Major in root position
   d) the Dominant seventh chord of c sharp minor harmonic in 2nd inversion
   e) the Dominant seventh chord of G flat Major in 3rd inversion
   f) the Dominant seventh chord of a minor harmonic in 1st inversion

| | a) | b) | c) | d) | e) | f) |
|---|---|---|---|---|---|---|
| Symbol: | $V_3^4$ | $V_5^6$ | $V^7$ | $V_3^4$ | $V_2^4$ | $V_5^6$ |

## DOMINANT 7th CHORDS in OPEN POSITION

**DOMINANT 7th chords in OPEN POSITION** are written on one staff or on the Grand Staff. The chord is spread out over more than an octave. Open Position and Closed Position Chords use the same chord symbols. The position of a chord is determined by the lowest note. The UPPER notes may be written in ANY order and do not affect the position of the chord.

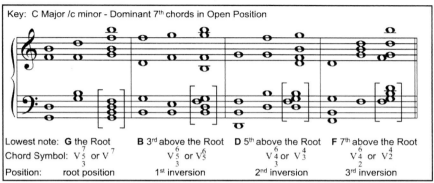

Key: C Major /c minor - Dominant 7th chords in Open Position

| Lowest note: | **G** the Root | **B** 3rd above the Root | **D** 5th above the Root | **F** 7th above the Root |
|---|---|---|---|---|
| Chord Symbol: | $V^7_5$ or $V^7$ | $V^6_5$ or $V^6_5$ | $V^6_4$ or $V^4_3$ | $V^6_4$ or $V^4_2$ |
| Position: | root position | 1st inversion | 2nd inversion | 3rd inversion |

1. For each of the following Dominant 7th chords, name:
   a) the Root. Write the chord in root position in [square brackets].
   b) the key to which it belongs.
   c) the position (root position, 1st inv, 2nd inv or 3rd inv); the chord symbol ( $V^7$, $V^6_5$, $V^4_3$ or $V^4_2$ ).

| | | | | | |
|---|---|---|---|---|---|
| a) Root: | C | F# | C | C# | B♭ |
| b) Key: | f min | b min | F Maj | f# min | E♭ Maj |
| c) Position: | 3rd inv | 2nd inv | 3rd inv | 1st inv | root |
| Symbol: | $V^4_2$ | $V^4_3$ | $V^4_2$ | $V^6_5$ | $V^7$ |

2. Add accidentals to each of the following chords to form Dominant 7th chords. Name the keys to which it belongs (Major and minor).

| B♭ Maj / b♭ min | F Maj / f min | A Maj / a min | D Maj / d min | G Maj / g min |
|---|---|---|---|---|

## DIMINISHED SEVENTH CHORDS

The **DIMINISHED SEVENTH** chord is a four note chord that is built on the raised seventh degree of a harmonic minor scale. It consists of a Root, minor 3, diminished 5 and a diminished 7. The symbol for the **diminished 7th** chord is vii°7. The Roman Numeral vii indicates the seventh degree above the Tonic. The number 7 after the Roman Numeral ( vii°7 ) indicates the Leading note (diminished) triad with an interval of a diminished 7th above the Root. The distance between each interval is a minor 3.

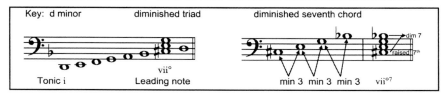

♫ **Note:** The raised 7th note is a diatonic semitone BELOW the Tonic of the harmonic minor key.
A root position diminished 7th chord is written as all line notes or all space notes.

1. For each of the following minor keys, write the diminished seventh chord in root position. Use accidentals. Use whole notes.

b minor     a minor     d minor     e♭ minor     g minor     f♯ minor

When using a Key Signature, an accidental is used to raise the 7th note, the Root of the chord.

♫ **Note:** The raised 7th note is the Root of a diminished 7th chord.
The raised 7th note is the third above the Root of a Dominant 7th chord.

2. Name the minor key to which the following diminished seventh chords belong.

a♭ minor    d minor    e minor    b♭ minor    c minor    g♯ minor

♫ **Note:** The abbreviation for Dominant 7th is Dom 7th or V7.
The abbreviation for diminished 7th is dim 7th or vii°7.

3. a) Name the following chords as a Dominant 7th ( V7 ) or a diminished 7th ( vii°7 ) chord.
   b) Name the minor key to which each chord belongs.

a)   dim 7th, vii°7    Dom 7th, V7    dim 7th, vii°7    Dom 7th, V7    Dom 7th, V7    dim 7th, vii°7

b)   c♯ minor    b minor    a♯ minor    d♯ minor    a minor    f minor

**THREE COMBINATIONS of DIMINISHED 7th CHORDS**

There are only **THREE COMBINATIONS** of a **DIMINISHED 7th CHORD**. When a diminished 7th chord is inverted, some notes will be changed to their enharmonic equivalent, creating the root position diminished 7th (vii°7) chord of another minor key.

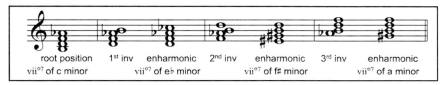

| root position | 1st inv | enharmonic | 2nd inv | enharmonic | 3rd inv | enharmonic |
|---|---|---|---|---|---|---|
| vii°7 of c minor | | vii°7 of e♭ minor | | vii°7 of f♯ minor | | vii°7 of a minor |

Five different root position diminished 7th chords can be built using the 4 notes on the keyboard of one diminished 7th chord. The notes will be used in different orders (inversions). Two diminished 7th chords will be enharmonic equivalents (same pitch/keys on the keyboard, different letter names).

There are **3 enharmonic minor keys**: g♯/a♭, d♯/e♭ and a♯/b♭.

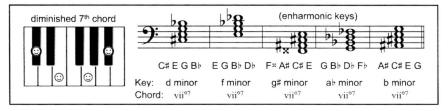

| | | (enharmonic keys) | | |
|---|---|---|---|---|
| C♯ E G B♭ | E G B♭ D♭ | F× A♯ C♯ E | G B♭ D♭ F♭ | A♯ C♯ E G |
| Key:   d minor | f minor | g♯ minor | a♭ minor | b minor |
| Chord:   vii°7 | vii°7 | vii°7 | vii°7 | vii°7 |

1. Identify the minor key for each of the following diminished 7th chords. Label each vii°7 chord.

diminished 7th chord

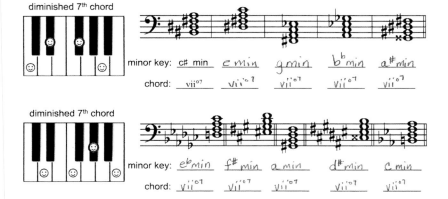

minor key:   c♯ min    e min    g min    b♭ min    a♯ min

chord:   vii°7    vii°7    vii°7    vii°7    vii°7

diminished 7th chord

minor key:   e♭ min    f♯ min    a min    d♯ min    c min

chord:   vii°7    vii°7    vii°7    vii°7    vii°7

♫ **Note:** The type/quality of a triad is Major, minor, Augmented or Diminished. The type/quality of a Dominant 7th chord or a diminished 7th chord is Dominant 7th or diminished 7th.

## POLYCHORD, QUARTAL CHORD and CLUSTER CHORD

A **POLYCHORD** is a combination of two or more different chords. They can be in root position or in any inversion. The chords may have notes in common, or none at all.

A **QUARTAL CHORD** is built on intervals of fourths. The fourths can be a combination of Perfect, Augmented and/or diminished. The Quartal chord has three or more notes.

 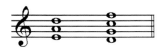

A **CLUSTER CHORD** or **TONE CLUSTER** is a chord consisting of three or more adjacent notes of a scale.

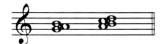

1. Identify the following chords as polychord, quartal chord or cluster chord.

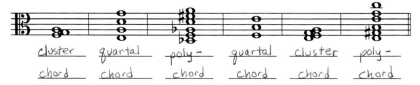

cluster chord    quartal chord    poly-chord    quartal chord    cluster chord    poly-chord

2. Match each chord description with the correct chord.

quartal chord     _C_

Dominant 7th chord     _e_

polychord     _a_

diminished 7th chord     _b_

cluster chord     _d_

a)

b)

c)

d)

e)

# Lesson 6          Review Test

Total Score: ____
100

Write the Circle of Fifths on a blank piece of paper. Use it as a reference when doing the review test.

**1.** a) Write the following melodic intervals BELOW the given notes. Use whole notes.

| Aug 6 | min 3 | Per 12 | dim 7 | Maj 2 |

b) Invert the above intervals in the Treble Clef. Use whole notes. Name the inversions.

dim 3      Maj 6      Per 4      Aug 2      min 7

**2.** For each of the following seventh chords, name:
a) the key to which each chord belongs (Major or minor).
b) the type (Dominant seventh, V⁷, or diminished seventh, vii°⁷ ).
c) the position (root, 1ˢᵗ inversion, 2ⁿᵈ inversion or 3ʳᵈ inversion).

a) e minor      g minor      c# minor      a minor      Db Major

b) Dom⁷ᵗʰ, V⁷    dim⁷ᵗʰ, vii°⁷   Dom⁷ᵗʰ, V⁷    dim⁷ᵗʰ, vii°⁷   Dom⁷ᵗʰ, V⁷

c) 2ⁿᵈ inv      root      3ʳᵈ inv      root      3ʳᵈ inv

**3.** For each of the following triads, name:
a) the Root.
b) the type/quality (Major, minor, Augmented or diminished).
c) the position (root, 1ˢᵗ inversion or 2ⁿᵈ inversion).

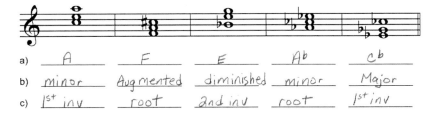

a)    A         F         E         Ab        Cb

b)  minor    Augmented   diminished   minor    Major

c)  1ˢᵗ inv    root      2nd inv     root     1ˢᵗ inv

**4.** Name the key of the following melody.

    a) Transpose the given melody **UP** a diminished 4 in the Bass Clef. Use the correct Key Signature. Name the new key.

<u>10</u>  b) Rewrite the given melody at the **SAME PITCH** in the Tenor Clef. Use the correct Key Signature.

Key: <u>D Major</u>

a)

Key: <u>G♭ Major</u>

b)

**5.** Write the Basic Beat and the pulse below each measure. Add rests below each bracket to complete the measure. Cross off the Basic Beat as each beat is completed.

<u>10</u>

72

**6.** For each of the following cadences, name:
   a) the key and chord symbols (V-I, iv-i, I-V, etc.).
   b) the type (Perfect, Plagal or Imperfect).

10

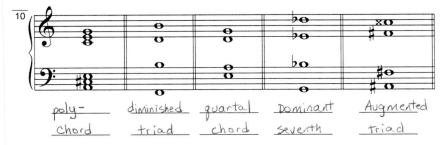

a) B♭Major   IV   V      a) c minor   i   V      a) b minor   iv   i
b) Imperfect            b) Imperfect            b) Plagal

**7.** Match each musical term with its English definition. (Not all definitions will be used.)

10

| Term | | Definition |
|---|---|---|
| largo | e | a) but |
| ritardando, rit. | i | b) above |
| ottava, 8ᵛᵃ | k | c) second; second or lower part of a duet |
| ma | a | d) not too much |
| meno | g | e) very slow |
| sopra | b | f) with expression |
| comodo | h | g) less |
| secondo, seconda | c | h) at a comfortable, easy tempo |
| non troppo | d | i) slowing down gradually |
| con espressione | f | j) quiet, tranquil |
| | | k) the interval of an octave |

**8.** Identify the following chords as: Augmented triad, diminished triad, Dominant seventh, diminished seventh, polychord or quartal chord.

10

poly-chord     diminished triad     quartal chord     Dominant seventh     Augmented triad

73

**9.** Write the following scales, ascending and descending, in the clefs indicated. Use whole notes.
   a) enharmonic Tonic minor, melodic form, of B flat Major using the correct Key Signature
   b) f minor harmonic, from Leading note to Leading note, using the correct Key Signature
   c) whole tone scale starting on G using accidentals
   d) Lydian mode starting on F flat using any standard notation

a)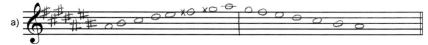

b)

c)

d)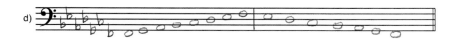

**10.** Analyze the following piece of music by answering the questions below.

**Allegretto**

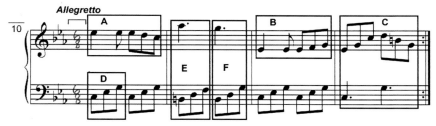

a) Add the correct Time Signature directly on the music.

b) Name the key of this piece. _c minor_

c) Circle the term for the relationship between the letter **A** and **B**: sequence  imitation  (inversion)

d) Name the cadence at the letter **C**. _Imperfect_

e) For the chord at **D**, name: Root: _C_ Type/Quality: _minor_ Position: _root_

f) For the chord at **E**, name: Root: _B♮_ Type/Quality: _dim 7th_ Position: _root_

g) For the chord at **F**, name: Root: _G_ Type/Quality: _Major_ Position: _1st inv_

h) Name the scale which contains all of these chords. _c minor harmonic_

i) Explain the B natural in this piece. _raised 7th note of c minor harmonic_

j) Explain the meaning of **Allegretto**. _fairly fast (a little slower than allegro)_

## Lesson 7    Writing a Cadence in Keyboard Style

**A CADENCE in KEYBOARD STYLE** is written with the Root of each triad in the Bass Clef and the Root, 3rd and 5th notes of each triad in the Treble Clef. A cadence is often written over 2 measures.

| Cadence | Major keys | minor keys |
|---|---|---|
| Perfect (authentic): | V - I | V - i |
| Plagal: | IV - I | iv - i |
| Imperfect (half cadence): | I - V, IV - V | i - V, iv - V |

Final cadence ends on the Tonic, a non final cadence ends on the Dominant.

♫ **Note:** In all cadences (except IV-V and iv- V) there is one note that is the same in both triads. This is called the **COMMON NOTE**. (When possible, it is written at the same pitch.)

When writing a Perfect cadence in keyboard style BELOW a melodic fragment, follow these 3 steps:

1. Name the key. Label the Perfect cadence (**V - I**). Write the note names below the triad.
2. Underline the bass notes and write them in the Bass Clef. (Same note value as the melody.)
3. Write the two remaining notes of each triad in the Treble Clef BELOW the given melody.

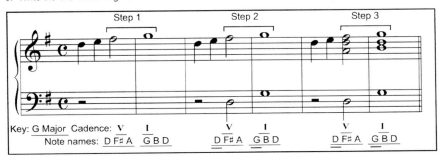

Key: G Major  Cadence:  **V    I**        **V    I**        **V    I**
     Note names:  D F♯ A   G B D      D F♯ A   G B D      D F♯ A   G B D

1. As in the example above, write a Perfect cadence in keyboard style BELOW the bracketed notes:
   a) Name the key. Label the Perfect cadence (**V - I**). Write the note names below the triad.
   b) Underline the bass notes and write them in the Bass Clef. (Same note value as the melody.)
   c) Write the two remaining notes of each triad in the Treble Clef BELOW the given melody.

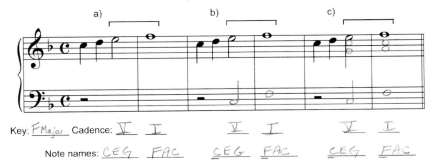

Key: F Major  Cadence:  V    I           V    I           V    I
     Note names:  C E G   F A C      C E G   F A C      C E G   F A C

## PERFECT CADENCES - MAJOR KEY (V - I) and MINOR KEY (V - i)

When **WRITING a PERFECT CADENCE**, identify the key based on the given melodic fragment. In a minor key, the Perfect cadence (**V - i**) will contain the raised 7th note of the harmonic minor.

♫ **Note:** The notes in the Treble Clef triads must be written in CLOSE POSITION (as close together as possible, either in root position, 1st inversion or 2nd inversion) below the given note.

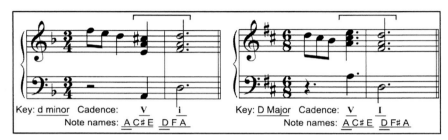

Key: d minor  Cadence: __V__  __i__
        Note names: _A C♯ E_  _D F A_

Key: D Major  Cadence: __V__  __I__
        Note names: _A C♯ E_  _D F♯ A_

1. Write a Perfect cadence in keyboard style BELOW the bracketed notes following these steps:

a) Name the key. Label the Perfect cadence **V-I** or **V-i**. Write the note names below the triad.

b) Underline the bass notes and write them in the Bass Clef.

c) Write the two remaining notes of each triad in the Treble Clef BELOW the given melody.

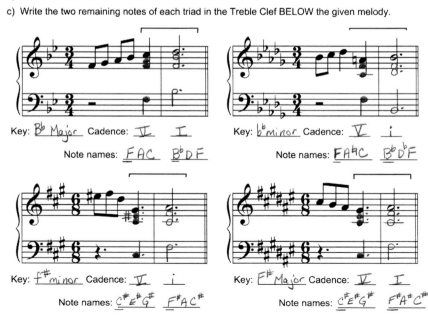

Key: B♭ Major  Cadence: __V__  __I__
        Note names: _F A C_  _B♭ D F_

Key: b♭ minor  Cadence: __V__  __i__
        Note names: _F A♮ C_  _B♭ D♭ F_

Key: f♯ minor  Cadence: __V__  __i__
        Note names: _C♯ E♯ G♯_  _F♯ A C♯_

Key: F♯ Major  Cadence: __V__  __I__
        Note names: _C♯ E♯ G♯_  _F♯ A♯ C♯_

76

## PLAGAL CADENCES - MAJOR KEY (IV - I) and MINOR KEY (iv - i)

When **WRITING a PLAGAL CADENCE**, identify the key based on the given melodic fragment. In a minor key, the Plagal cadence (**iv - i**) will NOT contain the raised 7th note of the harmonic minor.

♫ **Note:** The bass note may move up a Perfect 5 or down a Perfect 4 to the Tonic.
The notes in the Treble Clef are written BELOW the given notes.

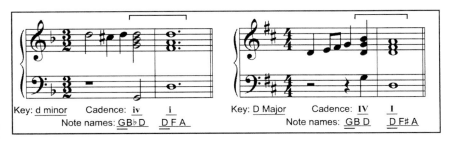

Key: d minor     Cadence: **iv**     **i**
Note names: GB♭D    D F A

Key: D Major     Cadence: **IV**     **I**
Note names: GB D    D F♯ A

1. Write a Plagal cadence in keyboard style BELOW the bracketed notes following these steps:

a) Name the key. Label the Plagal cadence **IV- I** or **iv-i**. Write the note names below the triad.

b) Underline the bass notes and write them in the Bass Clef.

c) Write the two remaining notes of each triad in the Treble Clef BELOW the given melody.

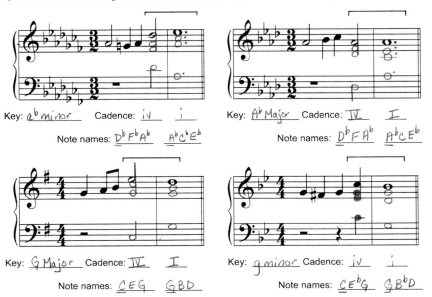

Key: a♭ minor     Cadence: iv     i
Note names: D♭ F♭ A♭     A♭ C♭ E♭

Key: A♭ Major     Cadence: IV     I
Note names: D♭ F A♭     A♭ C E♭

Key: G Major     Cadence: IV     I
Note names: C E G     G B D

Key: g minor     Cadence: iv     i
Note names: C E♭ G     G B♭ D

77

## IMPERFECT CADENCES - MAJOR KEY (I - V) and MINOR KEY (i - V)

When **WRITING an IMPERFECT CADENCE**, identify the key based on the given melodic fragment. In a minor key, the Imperfect cadence (**i - V**) will contain the raised 7th note of the harmonic minor.

♩ **Note:** A melody written in a minor key may or may not include the raised 7th note of the harmonic minor. If there is no raised 7th, look at the given notes of the cadence to determine if they belong to the I, IV or V triads of the Major key or the i, iv or V triads of the relative minor

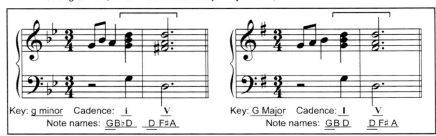

Key: g minor    Cadence: _i_    _V_
       Note names: GB♭D    D F♯A

Key: G Major    Cadence: _I_    _V_
       Note names: GB D    D F♯A

1. Write an Imperfect cadence in keyboard style BELOW the bracketed notes following these steps:
a) Name the key. Label the Imperfect cadence **I-V** or **i-V**. Write the note names below the triad.
b) Underline the bass notes and write them in the Bass Clef.
c) Write the two remaining notes of each triad in the Treble Clef BELOW the given melody.

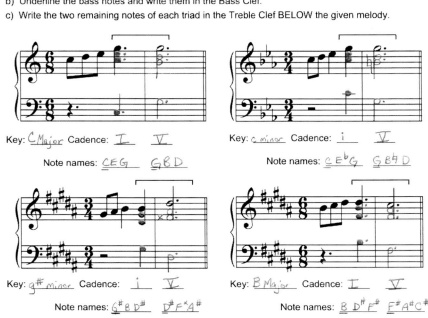

Key: C Major Cadence: _I_    _V_
       Note names: _C E G_    _G B D_

Key: c minor Cadence: _i_    _V_
       Note names: _C E♭ G_    _G B♮ D_

Key: g♯ minor Cadence: _i_    _V_
       Note names: _G♯ B D♯_    _D♯ F×A♯_

Key: B Major Cadence: _I_    _V_
       Note names: _B D♯ F♯_    _F♯ A♯ C♯_

## IMPERFECT CADENCES - MAJOR KEY (IV - V) and MINOR KEY (iv- V)

When **WRITING an IMPERFECT CADENCE**, identify the key based on the given melodic fragment. In a minor key, the Imperfect cadence (iv - V) will contain the raised 7th note of the harmonic minor.

♫ **Note:** There is NO common note in the IV - V (iv - V) Imperfect cadence. The Treble Clef notes move in contrary motion to the Bass Clef notes. Bass notes ASCEND (move up a Major 2); Treble Clef notes DESCEND (move down).

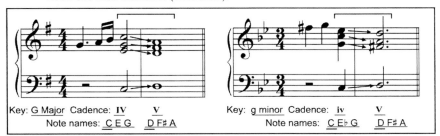

Key: G Major   Cadence: **IV**   **V**
Note names: _C E G_   _D F♯ A_

Key: g minor   Cadence: **iv**   **V**
Note names: _C E♭ G_   _D F♯ A_

1. Write an Imperfect cadence in keyboard style BELOW the bracketed notes following these steps:
a) Name the key. Label the Imperfect cadence **IV-V** or **iv-V**. Write the note names below the triad.
b) Underline the bass notes and write them in the Bass Clef (ascending a Major 2).
c) Write the two remaining notes of each triad in the Treble Clef BELOW the given melody.

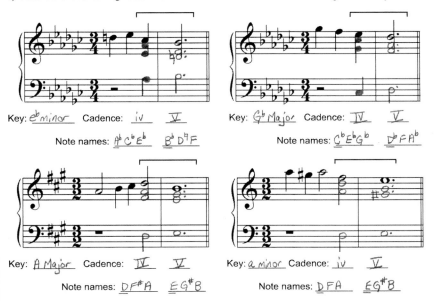

Key: e♭ minor   Cadence: iv   V
Note names: A♭ C♭ E♭   B♭ D♮ F

Key: G♭ Major   Cadence: IV   V
Note names: C♭ E♭ G♭   D♭ F A♭

Key: A Major   Cadence: IV   V
Note names: D F♯ A   E G♯ B

Key: a minor   Cadence: iv   V
Note names: D F A   E G♯ B

79

## PERFECT, PLAGAL and IMPERFECT CADENCES

When writing a **PERFECT, PLAGAL or IMPERFECT CADENCE** in keyboard style, the given melodic fragment will contain notes from the I, i, IV, iv or V chords.

To write a cadence in keyboard style below the bracketed notes, follow these 5 steps:
1. Name the key. Write the note names for the triads: I (i) _____, IV (iv) _____ and V _____.
2. Look at the notes under the bracket. Find the note in the I (i), IV (iv) or V chord. Write the chord symbols and note names for the cadence below the staff.
3. Underline the bass notes and write them in the Bass Clef. (Same note value as the melody.)
4. Write the two remaining notes of each triad in the Treble Clef BELOW the given melody.
5. Name the type of cadence (Perfect, Plagal or Imperfect).

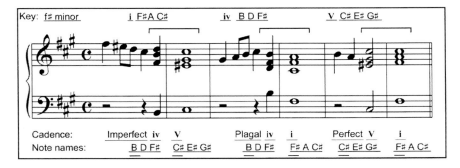

| Cadence: | Imperfect iv | V | Plagal iv | i | Perfect V | i |
|---|---|---|---|---|---|---|
| Note names: | B D F♯ | C♯ E♯ G♯ | B D F♯ | F♯ A C♯ | C♯ E♯ G♯ | F♯ A C♯ |

1. Write a cadence in keyboard style BELOW the bracketed notes following these steps:
   a) Name the key. Write the note names for the triads I (i), IV (iv) and V.
   b) Write the chord symbols and note names for the cadence below the staff.
   c) Underline the bass notes and write them in the Bass Clef.
   d) Write the two remaining notes of each triad in the Treble Clef BELOW the given melody.
   e) Name the type of cadence (Perfect, Plagal or Imperfect).

| Cadence: | Plagal iv | i | Imperfect iv | V | Perfect V | i |
|---|---|---|---|---|---|---|
| Note names: | F A♭ C | C E♭ G | F A♭ C | G B♮ D | G B♮ D | C E♭ G |

## PERFECT, PLAGAL and IMPERFECT CADENCES

1. For each melodic fragment, write a cadence in keyboard style BELOW the bracketed notes.
   a) Name the key. Write the note names for the triads I (i), IV (iv) and V.
   b) Name the type of cadence (Perfect, Plagal or Imperfect) and write the chord symbols.
   c) Name the notes in each of the triads of the cadence.

a) Key: F minor    i  F A♭ C    iv  B♭ D♭ F    V  C E♮ G

b) Cadence: Imperfect  iv  V    Plagal  iv  i    Perfect  V  i

c) Note names:   B♭ D♭ F   C E♮ G    B♭ D♭ F   F A♭ C    C E♮ G   F A♭ C
                                                              (for Imperfect i  V )

a) Key: d♯ minor    i  D♯ F♯ A♯    iv  G♯ B D♯    V  A♯ C× E♯

b) Cadence: Plagal  iv  i    Imperfect iv  V    Perfect  V  i

c) Note names:  G♯ B D♯   D♯ F♯ A♯    G♯ B D♯   A♯ C× E♯    A♯ C× E♯   D♯ F♯ A♯

a) Key: B♭ Major    I  B♭ D F    IV  E♭ G B♭    V  F A C

b) Cadence: Imperfect  IV  V    Imperfect  I  V    Plagal  IV  I

c) Note names:  E♭ G B♭   F A C    B♭ D F   F A C    E♭ G B♭   B♭ D F

## PERFECT CADENCES USING THE V7 CHORD

Chords: V7      V7      V7

A **V7 Chord** is the Dominant triad plus a minor 7th.

A PERFECT Major Cadence is a **V - I** or **V7 - I** chord progression.
A PERFECT minor cadence is a **V - i** or **V7 - i** chord progression.

When a Dominant 7th (**V7**) chord is used in a Perfect Cadence, the 5th note above the Dominant may be omitted. The **V7** chord ALWAYS contains the added 7th note. The **V7** chord contains a tritone.

♫ **Note:** The raised 7th note "hugs" the Dominant note (interval of a 2nd).

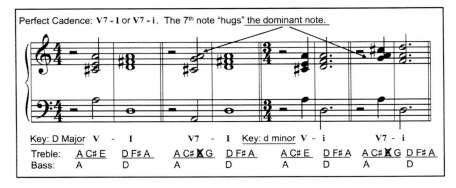

Perfect Cadence: **V7 - I** or **V7 - i**. The 7th note "hugs" the dominant note.

| | Key: D Major V - I | V7 - I | Key: d minor V - i | V7 - i |
|---|---|---|---|---|
| Treble: | A C# E  D F# A | A C# ~~E~~ G  D F# A | A C# E  D F# A | A C# ~~E~~ G  D F# A |
| Bass: | A      D | A      D | A      D | A      D |

1. Name the key. Use chord symbols to identify the following Perfect Cadences.
   Major keys: **V - I** or **V7 - I**. Minor keys: **V - i** or **V7 - i**.

Key: <u>Ab Major</u> V7 - I  <u>Bb Major</u> V - I  <u>c# minor</u> V7 - i

Key: <u>g minor</u> V - i  <u>f# minor</u> V7 - i  <u>Db Major</u> V7 - I

# Lesson 7       Review Test

Total Score: _____
/100

Write the Circle of Fifths on a blank piece of paper. Use it as a reference when doing the review test.

**1.** a) Name the following harmonic intervals.

Maj 9    Aug 6    min 2    dim 3    Aug 4

b) Invert the above intervals in the Bass Clef. Use whole notes. Name the inversions.

min 7    dim 3    Maj 7    Aug 6    dim 5

**2.** Add the necessary accidentals to form Dominant seventh chords. For each chord, name:
     a) the keys to which it belongs (Major and minor).
     b) the position (root, 1st inversion, 2nd inversion or 3rd inversion).

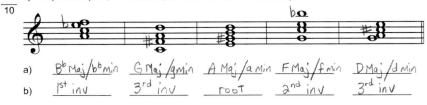

a)   Bb Maj/bb min   G Maj/g min   A Maj/a min   F Maj/f min   D Maj/d min

b)   1st inv     3rd inv     root     2nd inv     3rd inv

**3.** For each of the following triads, name:
     a) the Root.
     b) the type/quality (Major, minor, Augmented or diminished).
     c) the position (root, 1st inversion or 2nd inversion).

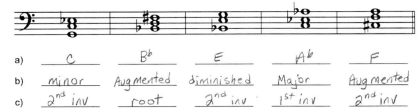

a)    C     Bb     E     Ab     F

b)   minor   Augmented   diminished   Major   Augmented

c)   2nd inv   root   2nd inv   1st inv   2nd inv

**4.** a) Name the key of the following melody. Transpose it **UP** a minor sixth in the Bass Clef. Use the correct Key Signature. Name the new key.

**Scherzando**

Key: _D Major_

Scherzando

Key: _B♭ Major_

b) Name the key of the following melody. Rewrite the given melody at the **SAME PITCH** in the Alto Clef. Use the correct Key Signature.

Key: _A♭ Major_

**5.** Write the Basic Beat and the pulse below each measure. Add rests below each bracket to complete the measure. Cross off the Basic Beat as each beat is completed.

Basic Beat:

Pulse:

Basic Beat:

Pulse:

**6.** a) Name the key for the following melodic fragments. Write a cadence (keyboard style) **BELOW** the given bracketed notes. Use chord symbols to identify the cadence. Name the type of cadence (Perfect, Plagal or Imperfect).

10  Key: d minor          i  D F A          iv  G B♭ D          I  A C# E

Cadence: Imperfect  i  V        Plagal  iv  i          Perfect  V  i
Note names:  DFA        AC#E      GB♭D    DFA          AC#E    DFA

b) Name the key for each of the following cadences. Use chord symbols to identify the cadence. Name the type of cadence (Perfect, Plagal or Imperfect).

Key: E♭ Major  V⁷ - I    Key: b minor  iv - V    Key: a# minor  V⁷ - i
Cadence: Perfect        Cadence: Imperfect     Cadence: Perfect

**7.** Match each musical term with its English definition. (Not all definitions will be used.)

| Term | | Definition |
|------|---|-----------|
10
| tempo | d | a) slow and solemn |
| prima volta | k | b) held, sustained |
| loco | h | c) smooth |
| grave | a | d) speed at which music is performed |
| tenuto | b | e) as fast as possible |
| volti subito, v.s. | j | f) the end |
| legato | c | g) left hand |
| mano sinistra, M.S. | g | h) return to the normal register |
| prestissimo | e | i) right hand |
| fine | f | j) turn the page quickly |
| | | k) first time |

**8.** Match each description with the correct chord.

| Description | | Chord |
|---|---|---|
| cluster chord | _b_ | a) 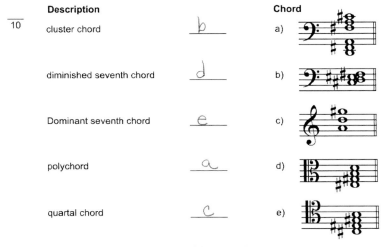 |
| diminished seventh chord | _d_ | b) |
| Dominant seventh chord | _e_ | c) |
| polychord | _a_ | d) |
| quartal chord | _c_ | e) |

f) Circle the scale which contains all of these chords:

b minor melodic      d♯ minor natural      (f♯ minor harmonic)

**9.** Write the following scales, ascending and descending, in the clefs indicated. Use whole notes.
a) enharmonic Tonic Major of g sharp minor using the correct Key Signature
b) Dorian mode starting on G sharp using any standard notation
10   c) chromatic scale starting on F sharp using any standard notation
d) Mixolydian mode starting on B flat using any standard notation

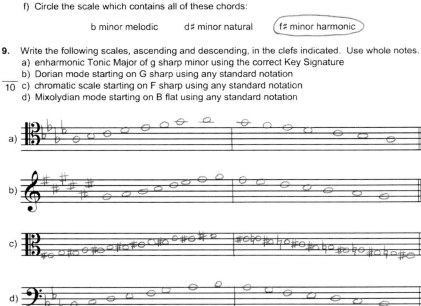

**10.** Analyze the following excerpt by answering the questions below.

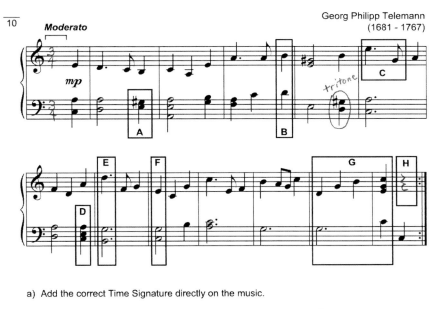

a) Add the correct Time Signature directly on the music.

b) Name the intervals at the letters: **A** _Major 3_ **B** _Major 6_ **C** _Major 6_

c) Circle and label one example of a tritone directly on the music. Name the interval. _Aug 4_

d) For the chord at **D**, name: Root: _A_ Type/Quality: _minor_ Position: _1st inv_

e) For the chord at **E**, name: Root: _G_ Type/Quality: _Major_ Position: _1st inv_

f) For the chord at **F**, name: Root: _C_ Type/Quality: _Major_ Position: _root_

g) Name the type of cadence formed by the chords at the letter **G**. _Perfect_

h) Add the appropriate rest(s) to complete the measure at the letter **H**.

i) Explain the meaning of **_Moderato_**. _moderate tempo_

j) How many measures are in this piece? _12_

# Lesson 8    Rhythm - Simple, Compound and Hybrid Time

**HYBRID TIME** (Mixed Meter) is a combination of Simple Time (Basic Beat is one undotted note) and Compound Time (Compound Basic Beat is one dotted note). Hybrid meter can be in duple, triple or quadruple time. The **TOP** number is **5, 7, 9, 10** or **11**. The **BOTTOM** number is **2, 4, 8** or **16**.

### HYBRID DUPLE TIME

In Hybrid **DUPLE** Time the **TOP** number is always **5**. The 5 pulses are grouped as follows:

| | | | | | |
|---|---|---|---|---|---|
| **TWO** Groups of : | 3 | 2 | **OR** | 2 | 3 |
| Pulse: | S w w | M w | **OR** | S w | M w w |
| Hybrid Pulse: | S· | w | **OR** | S | w· |

♫ **Note:** Use the same pattern of 3-2 or 2-3 to complete each rhythm.

1. Following the examples, write the Basic Beat, pulse and Hybrid pulse under each measure. Add bar lines to complete the following rhythms.

# HYBRID TRIPLE TIME

In **HYBRID TRIPLE TIME**, when **7** is the top number in the Time Signature, the 7 Basic Beats will combine into one dotted and two undotted Hybrid Pulses.

♩ **Note:** A dotted note will be used for one dotted Hybrid pulse.

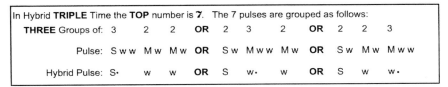

In Hybrid **TRIPLE** Time the **TOP** number is **7**. The 7 pulses are grouped as follows:

| THREE Groups of: | 3 | 2 | 2 | OR | 2 | 3 | 2 | OR | 2 | 2 | 3 |
|---|---|---|---|---|---|---|---|---|---|---|---|
| Pulse: | S w w | M w | M w | OR | S w | M w w | M w | OR | S w | M w | M w w |
| Hybrid Pulse: | S· | w | w | OR | S | w· | w | OR | S | w | w· |

♩ **Note:** Use the same pattern of 3-2-2 or 2-3-2 or 2-2-3 to complete each rhythm.

1. Following the examples, write in the Basic Beat, pulse and Hybrid pulse under each measure. Add bar lines to complete the following rhythms.

## HYBRID QUADRUPLE TIME

| In Hybrid **QUADRUPLE** Time the **TOP** number is **9**, **10** or **11**. The pulses are grouped as follows: | | | | | | |
|---|---|---|---|---|---|---|
| **FOUR** Groups of: | 3 | 2 | 2 | 2 | equals 9 | Pulses can also be combined: |
| Pulse: | S w w | M w | M w | M w | | 2-3-2-2 or 2-2-3-2 or 2-2-2-3 |
| Hybrid Pulse: | S· | w | M | w | | |
| **FOUR** Groups of: | 3 | 2 | 3 | 2 | equals 10 | Pulses can also be combined: |
| Pulse: | S w w | M w | M w w | M w | | 3-3-2-2 or 3-2-2-3 or 2-3-2-3 |
| Hybrid Pulse: | S· | w | M· | w | | or 2-3-3-2 or 2-2-3-3 |
| **FOUR** Groups of: | 3 | 3 | 3 | 2 | equals 11 | Pulses can also be combined: |
| Pulse: | S w w | M w w | M w w | M w | | 3-2-3-3 or 3-3-2-3 or 2-3-3-3 |
| Hybrid Pulse: | S· | w· | M· | w | | |

♫ **Note:** Use the same pattern of 2's and 3's to complete each rhythm.

1. Following the examples, write in the Basic Beat, pulse and Hybrid pulse under each measure. Add bar lines to complete the following rhythms.

## TIME SIGNATURES and RESTS in HYBRID TIME

When adding **TIME SIGNATURES** in Hybrid Time, look for groups and determine the Basic Beat.

♫ **Note:** Notes held for a full measure must be written as tied notes.

1. Write the Basic Beat and Hybrid Beat (dotted note or undotted note) below each measure.
   Add the correct Time Signature below the bracket for each of the following rhythms.

When adding **RESTS** to Hybrid Time, determine the pattern of Strong and weak beats. A dotted rest is only used when completing a group of three pulses: one Compound Basic Beat = one dotted rest.

♫ **Note:** Rests are combined for: **S + w** or **M + w** or **S· + w·** or **M· + w·**
   A **dotted** pulse **CANNOT** be combined with an **undotted** pulse.
   **S· ~ w** or **M· ~ w** or **S ~ w·** or **M ~ w·**

2. Add rests below each bracket to complete the following measures. Cross off the Basic Beat as each beat is completed.

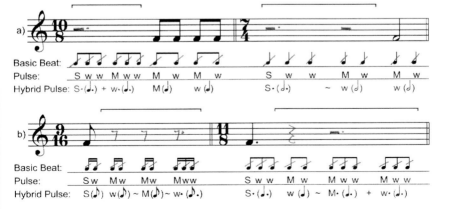

## WHOLE REST and DOTTED WHOLE REST in HYBRID TIME

A **WHOLE REST** fills ANY measure in Hybrid Time. An exception to the rule is Hybrid "**2**" time when a whole rest may fill a whole measure with silence OR it may receive 2 beats (**S + w** or **M + w**).

A **DOTTED WHOLE REST** is equal to 3 half notes and is used when completing a group of three half note Basic Beats. A dotted whole rest receives 3 beats (**S + w + w** or **M + w + w**).

♫ **Note:** Notes that are beamed together belong to the SAME Basic Beat.

1. Write the Basic Beat, pulse and Hybrid pulse below each measure. Add rests below each bracket to complete the measure. Cross off the Basic Beat as each beat is completed.

# Lesson 8     Review Test

Total Score: ____

100

Write the Circle of Fifths on a blank piece of paper. Use it as a reference when doing the review test.

**1.** a) Name the following harmonic intervals.

10

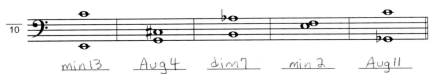

min13     Aug4     dim7     min2     Aug11

b) Invert the above intervals in the Tenor Clef. Use whole notes. Name the inversions.

Maj 3     dim 5     Aug 2     Maj 7     dim 5

**2.** For each of the following seventh chords, name:
a) the key to which each chord belongs (Major or minor).
b) the type (Dominant seventh, $V^7$ or diminished seventh, vii°7).

10  c) the position (root, 1st inversion, 2nd inversion or 3rd inversion).

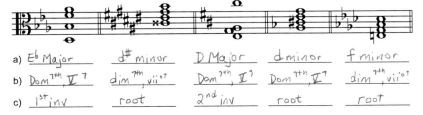

a) Eb Major     d# minor     D Major     d minor     f minor

b) Dom 7th, V 7     dim 7th, vii°7     Dom 7th, V 7     Dom 7th, V 7     dim 7th, vii°7

c) 1st inv     root     2nd inv     root     root

**3.** For each of the following triads, name:
a) the Root.
b) the type/quality (Major, minor, Augmented or diminished).

10  c) the position.
d) Name the scale which contains all these chords: ___g# minor harmonic___

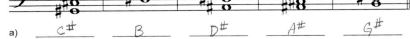

a)     c#     B     D#     A#     G#

b)     minor     Aug     Major     dim     min

c)     2nd inv     1st inv     2nd inv     root     1st inv

4. Name the key of the following melody. Transpose the given melody **UP** a diminished fifth in the Treble Clef. Use the correct key signature. Name the new key.

Key: D Major

Key: A♭ Major

5. Write the Basic Beat and the pulse below each measure. Add rests below each bracket to complete the measure. Cross off the Basic Beat as each beat is completed.

94

**6.** Write the following scales, ascending and descending, in the clefs indicated. Use the correct Key Signature. Use whole notes.

10

a) enharmonic relative minor, melodic form, of C flat Major
b) e flat minor harmonic, from supertonic to supertonic
c) b flat minor natural, from subdominant to subdominant
d) enharmonic Tonic Major of B Major
e) Lydian mode starting on G
f) Phrygian mode starting on C sharp

a)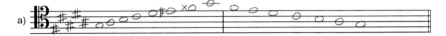

b)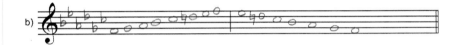

c)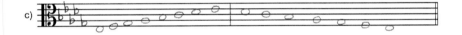

d)

e)

f)

**7.** a) Name the key for the following melodic fragments. Write a cadence (keyboard style) **BELOW** the bracketed notes. Name the type of cadence (Perfect, Plagal or Imperfect).

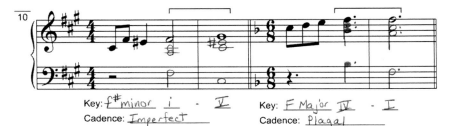

Key: f# minor   i   -   V      Key: F Major   IV   -   I

Cadence: Imperfect        Cadence: Plagal

b) Name the key for each of the following cadences. Use chord symbols to identify the cadence. Name the type of cadence (Perfect, Plagal or Imperfect).

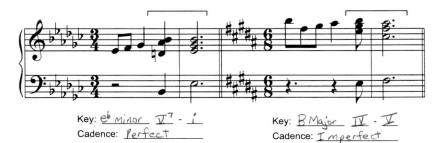

Key: eb minor   V⁷ - i      Key: B Major   IV - V

Cadence: Perfect        Cadence: Imperfect

**8.** Match each musical term with its English definition. (Not all definitions will be used.)

| Term | | Definition |
|---|---|---|
| martellato | h | a) becoming slower and softer |
| pesante | d | b) in a singing style |
| calando | a | c) majestic |
| sostenuto | j | d) weighty, with emphasis |
| andante | g | e) becoming quicker |
| rubato | k | f) sweet, gentle |
| accelerando, accel. | e | g) moderately slow; at a walking pace |
| cantabile | b | h) strongly accented, hammered |
| dolce | f | i) graceful |
| maestoso | c | j) sustained |
| | | k) with some freedom of tempo to enhance musical expression |

**9.** Add the correct Time Signature below the bracket for each of the following rhythms.

**10.** Analyze the following piece of music by answering the questions below.

a) Add the correct Time Signature directly on the music.

b) Name the key of this piece. _____ C Major _____

c) Name the intervals at the letters: **A** _min 6_ **B** _min 10_ **C** _min 13_

d) For the chord at **D**, name: Root: _C_ Type/Quality: _Major_ Position: _root_

e) Name the mode at the letter **E**. _Dorian_

f) For the chord at **F**, name: Root: _G_ Type/Quality: _Major_ Position: _1st inv_

g) Name the mode at the letter **G**. _Mixolydian_

h) Give the term for the relationship between the RH at measures 5 and 6. _sequence_

i) Name the type of cadence formed by the chords at the letter **H**. _V⁷-I Perfect_

j) Explain the meaning of **Andantino**. _a little faster than Andante (moderately slow)_

# Lesson 9      Transposition - Minor Key to Minor Key

**TRANSPOSITION** is when music is written or played at a different pitch.

When transposing from a **MINOR KEY to a MINOR KEY**, name the ORIGINAL key first. Start at the Tonic note and count **UP** or **DOWN** to determine the interval note name. That note names the Tonic of the NEW minor key. All the notes must move up or down the same interval.

♫ **Note:** Any notes using accidentals in the given melody must be transposed (raised or lowered) in the new melody using accidentals.

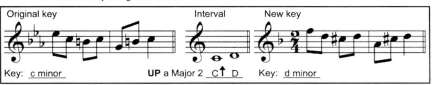

1. a) Name the key of the given melody.
   b) Write the interval of a melodic Major 2 ABOVE the Tonic note (B♭). Name the note.
   c) Name the new key. Transpose the given melody **UP** a Major 2 in the Treble Clef, using the correct Key Signature.

♫ **Note:** When a minor key is transposed to a new key, the new key will ALWAYS remain minor.

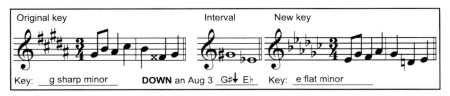

2. a) Name the key of the given melody.
   b) Write the interval of a melodic Aug 3 BELOW the Tonic note (C♯). Name the note.
   c) Name the new key. Transpose the given melody **DOWN** an Aug 3 in the Treble Clef, using the correct Key Signature.

## TRANSPOSING a MELODY with ACCIDENTALS

When **TRANSPOSING a MELODY with ACCIDENTALS**, if the original melody contains accidentals, the transposed melody will contain accidentals. If an accidental raises or lowers a note in the original melody, the transposed melody must contain an accidental to raise or lower the note as well.

♫ **Note:** When adding accidentals, observe the Key Signature. Example: Key of **e minor**, F♯ is lowered to F♮ and then raised to F♯ in the original key. Transposing to the new key of **a minor**, the same degree is the note B. B natural is lowered to B♭ and then raised to B♮.

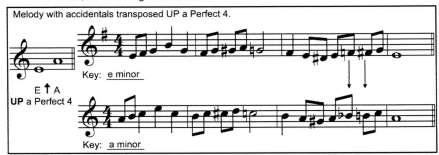

Melody with accidentals transposed UP a Perfect 4.

Key: e minor

E ↑ A
**UP** a Perfect 4

Key: a minor

♫ **Note:** When transposing a melody UP or DOWN to a new key, always determine the interval first. That note names the new key.

1.  The following melody is in the key of f minor. Transpose the melody and name the new key.
    a)  Transpose the given melody **UP** a Perfect 4, using the correct Key Signature.
    b)  Transpose the given melody **DOWN** a minor 2, using the correct Key Signature.

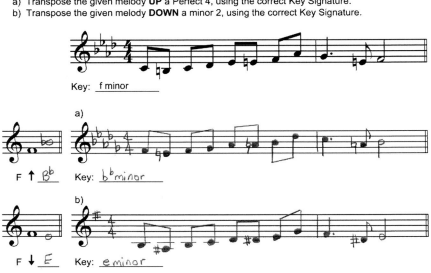

Key: f minor

a)

F ↑ B♭    Key: b♭minor

b)

F ↓ E    Key: e minor

# TRANSPOSING a MELODY - MAJOR KEY to MAJOR KEY and MINOR KEY to MINOR KEY

When **TRANSPOSING a MELODY** UP or DOWN an interval, write the interval ABOVE or BELOW the Tonic note of the given mélody as indicated. That note determines the new key.

♫ **Note:** Transpose a **MAJOR** key to a **MAJOR** key and a **MINOR** key to a **MINOR** key.

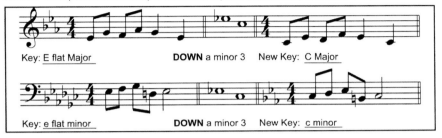

Key: E flat Major          **DOWN** a minor 3     New Key: __C Major__

Key: e flat minor          **DOWN** a minor 3     New Key: __c minor__

♫ **Note:** A double bar line cancels a Key Signature.

1. For each of the following:
   a) Name the key of the given melody.
   b) Write the Tonic note and the given interval ABOVE or BELOW the Tonic note as indicated.
   c) Name the new key. Transpose the melody UP or DOWN by the given interval, using the correct Key Signature.

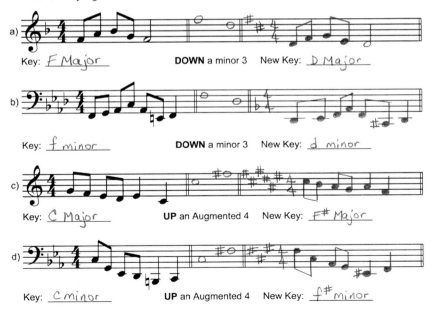

a)

Key: __F Major__           **DOWN** a minor 3     New Key: __D Major__

b)

Key: __f minor__           **DOWN** a minor 3     New Key: __d minor__

c)

Key: __C Major__           **UP** an Augmented 4   New Key: __F# Major__

d)

Key: __C minor__           **UP** an Augmented 4   New Key: __f# minor__

101

## TRANSPOSING a MELODY to a NEW KEY

When **TRANSPOSING a MELODY to a NEW KEY**, a Major key will ALWAYS remain a Major key and a minor key will ALWAYS remain a minor key. All the notes move UP or DOWN the SAME interval.

There are 2 possible keys for each melody: the Major Key and the relative minor key. If the 7th note of the minor key appears and it is raised, the key is minor. However, the 7th note of the minor key may not appear in the melody.

♫ **Note:** If there is no 7th note, look for the overall tonality: does the melody use more Tonic notes of the Major or minor key; is there a Tonic triad from the Major or minor key; is the final note the Tonic note of the Major or minor key? (The melody MAY NOT end on a Tonic note.)

(No raised 7th; c minor triad)

Key: __c minor__          **DOWN** a dim 4 __C ↓ G♯__          Key: __g♯ minor__

♫ **Note:** Draw a staff in the margin. Write the interval ABOVE or BELOW the Tonic note of the given melody as indicated. That note names the new key.

1. Name the key of the following melody. Transpose it **UP** an Augmented 2 in the Bass Clef, using the correct Key Signature. Name the new key.

Key: __B♭ Major__

Key: __C♯ Major__

2. Name the key of the following melody. Transpose it **UP** a minor 3 in the Treble Clef, using the correct Key Signature. Name the new key.

Key: __a minor__

Key: __C minor__

**TRANSPOSING a MELODY from CLEF to SAME CLEF**

When **TRANSPOSING a MELODY** from one key to another (Major to Major or minor to minor), the CLEF will remain the same.

♪ **Note:** Draw a staff in the margin. Use the SAME clef as the given melody. Write the interval ABOVE or BELOW the Tonic note as indicated. That note names the new key.

1. Name the key of the following melody. Transpose it **DOWN** a Major 2 in the Tenor Clef, using the correct Key Signature. Name the new key.

Key: C# minor

Key: b minor

2. Name the key of the following melody. Transpose it **UP** a minor 2 in the Alto Clef, using the correct Key Signature. Name the new key.

Key: f# minor

Key: g minor

3. Name the key of the following melody. Transpose it **DOWN** an Augmented 3 in the Alto Clef, using the correct Key Signature. Name the new key.

Key: B Major

Key: Gb Major

**TRANSPOSITION to CONCERT PITCH - ORCHESTRAL B flat INSTRUMENTS**

**CONCERT PITCH** (the note A) is the sounding pitch to which ALL instruments are tuned and the pitch that non-transposing instruments sound. **C** instruments (non-transposing instruments) such as the piano, violin or flute, sound pitches at the **SAME** level as the notes that are written on the staff.

The Orchestral B flat instruments (transposing instruments) such as the **B♭ Clarinet** and **B♭ Trumpet**, when playing C, actually produce the sound of B♭ (a Major 2 lower).

When transposing a melody written for B♭ Clarinet or B♭ Trumpet to concert pitch, transpose **DOWN** a Major 2.

written pitch   concert pitch

♫ **Note:** Music written for an Orchestral B flat instrument can be written in any Key, Major or minor.

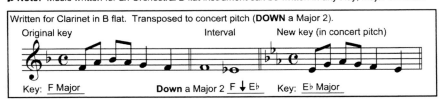

Written for Clarinet in B flat. Transposed to concert pitch (**DOWN** a Major 2).

Original key     Interval     New key (in concert pitch)

Key: _F Major_     **Down** a Major 2 _F ↓ E♭_     Key: _E♭ Major_

♫ **Note:** The words Trumpet and Clarinet both end with the 2 letters **et**.
"Hint": the instruments with **et** on the end go **DOWN** a Major 2.

1. The following melody is written for Clarinet in B flat. Name the key in which it is written. Transpose it to concert pitch, using the correct Key Signature. Name the new key.

Key: _E Major_     Down a Major 2 _E ↓ D_     Key: _D Major_

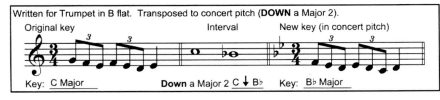

Written for Trumpet in B flat. Transposed to concert pitch (**DOWN** a Major 2).

Original key     Interval     New key (in concert pitch)

Key: _C Major_     **Down** a Major 2 _C ↓ B♭_     Key: _B♭ Major_

2. The following melody is written for Trumpet in B flat. Name the key in which it is written. Transpose it to concert pitch, using the correct Key Signature. Name the new key.

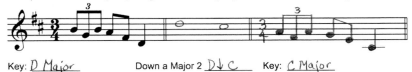

Key: _D Major_     Down a Major 2 _D ↓ C_     Key: _C Major_

## TRANSPOSITION to CONCERT PITCH - ORCHESTRAL F INSTRUMENTS

**ORCHESTRAL F INSTRUMENTS and ORCHESTRAL B FLAT INSTRUMENTS** indicate the key of the instrument NOT the key of the music it plays. Transposing music written for an orchestral instrument "in B flat" or "in F" to concert pitch indicates a specific interval based on the instrument.

The Orchestral F instruments (transposing instruments) such as the **English Horn** and **French Horn**, when playing C, actually produce the sound of F (a Perfect 5 lower).

When transposing a melody written for English Horn or French Horn in F to concert pitch, transpose **DOWN** a Perfect 5.

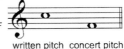

written pitch  concert pitch

♫ **Note:** Music written for an Orchestral F instrument can be written in any Key, Major or minor.

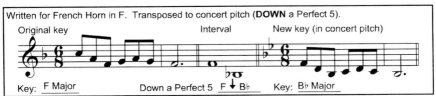

Written for French Horn in F. Transposed to concert pitch (**DOWN** a Perfect 5).

Original key          Interval          New key (in concert pitch)

Key: F Major          Down a Perfect 5  F ↓ B♭   Key: B♭ Major

♫ **Note:** The French Horn and English Horn are both Horns. "Horns" has 5 letters.
"Hint": the instruments that are Horns go **DOWN** a Perfect 5.

1. The following melody is written for French Horn in F. Name the key in which it is written. Transpose it to concert pitch, using the correct Key Signature. Name the new key.

Key: A Major          Down a Perfect 5  A ↓ D   Key: D Major

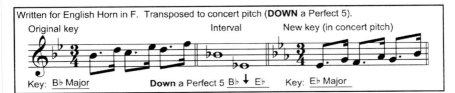

Written for English Horn in F. Transposed to concert pitch (**DOWN** a Perfect 5).

Original key          Interval          New key (in concert pitch)

Key: B♭ Major         **Down a Perfect 5** B♭ ↓ E♭  Key: E♭ Major

2. The following melody is written for English Horn in F. Name the key in which it is written. Transpose it to concert pitch, using the correct Key Signature. Name the new key.

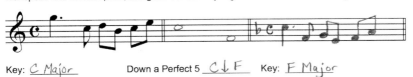

Key: C Major          Down a Perfect 5  C ↓ F   Key: F Major

## WRITTEN RANGE for ORCHESTRAL INSTRUMENTS

The **WRITTEN RANGE** for **ORCHESTRAL INSTRUMENTS** varies depending on the instrument. When transposing, each orchestral instrument has a specific range of sound.

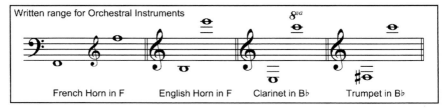

♫ **Note:** To transpose to concert pitch:
French Horn in F and English Horn in F (Horns) transposed DOWN a Perfect 5.
Clarinet in B♭ and Trumpet in B♭ (et) transposed DOWN a Major 2.

1.  The following melody is written for French Horn in F. Name the key in which it is written. Transpose it to concert pitch in the Bass Clef, using the correct Key Signature. Name the new key.

Key: _E♭ Major_

Key: _A♭ Major_

2.  The following melody is written for Clarinet in B flat. Name the key in which it is written. Transpose it to concert pitch in the Treble Clef, using the correct Key Signature. Name the new key.

Key: _B♭ Major_

Key: _A♭ Major_

# Lesson 9      Review Test

Total Score: ____
100

Write the Circle of Fifths on a blank piece of paper. Use it as a reference when doing the review test.

**1.**    a) Name the following melodic intervals.

10

_Aug 4_    _min 7_    _dim 3_    _Maj 6_    _dim 12_

b) Change the **LOWER** note of each interval **ENHARMONICALLY**. Rename the interval.

_dim 5_    _Aug 6_    _Maj 2_    _dim 7_    _Aug 11_

**2.**    For each of the following seventh chords, name:
     a) the key to which each chord belongs (Major or minor).
     b) the type (Dominant seventh, $V^7$, or diminished seventh, $vii^{o7}$ )
10    c) the position (root, 1st inversion, 2nd inversion or 3rd inversion).

a)   _g# minor_    _Bb Major_    _b minor_    _Ab Major_    _f# minor_

b)   _dim 7th, vii o7_   _Dom 7th, V7_   _dim 7th, vii o7_   _Dom 7th, V7_   _Dom 7th, V7_

c)   _root_    _1st inv_    _root_    _2nd inv_    _3rd inv_

**3.** Write the following triads using accidentals. Use whole notes.
Name the type/quality (Major, minor, Augmented or diminished).

10 a) the **LEADING NOTE** triad of C Major in second inversion
 b) the **SUBMEDIANT** triad of b flat minor harmonic in root position
 c) the **SUPERTONIC** triad of e flat minor harmonic in second inversion
 d) the **MEDIANT** triad of F Major in first inversion
 e) the **MEDIANT** triad of d minor harmonic in root position

Type: diminished   Major   diminished   minor   Augmented

**4.** a) The following melody is written for Trumpet in B flat. Name the key in which it is written.
Transpose it to concert pitch in the Treble Clef. Use the correct Key Signature.
Name the new key.

10

Key: g# minor

Key: f# minor

b) The following melody is written for English Horn in F. Name the key in which it is written.
Transpose it to concert pitch in the Treble Clef. Use the correct Key Signature.
Name the new key.

Key: Eb Major

Key: Ab Major

**5.** Write the Basic Beat and the pulse below each measure. Add rests below each bracket to complete the measure. Cross off the Basic Beat as each beat is completed.

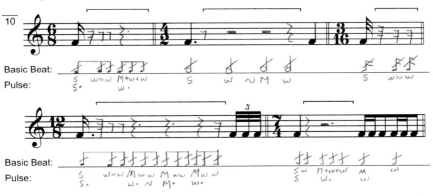

**6.** Identify the following scales as: Dorian, Phrygian, Lydian, Mixolydian, Aeolian, Major pentatonic, minor pentatonic, blues or whole tone.

**7.**  a)  Name the key for the following melodic fragments.  Use chord symbols to identify the cadence.  Write a cadence (keyboard style) **BELOW** the bracketed notes.  Name the type of cadence (Perfect, Plagal or Imperfect).

10

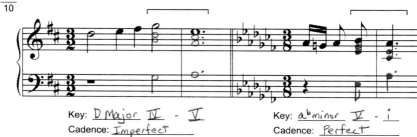

Key: D Major IV - V
Cadence: Imperfect

Key: a♭ minor V - i
Cadence: Perfect

b)  Name the key for each of the following cadences.  Use chord symbols to identify the cadence.  Name the type of cadence (Perfect, Plagal or Imperfect).

Key: a minor iv - i
Cadence: Plagal

Key: E♭ Major V⁷ - I
Cadence: Perfect

**8.**  Match each musical term with its English definition.  (Not all definitions will be used.)

10

| Term | | Definition |
|------|------|------|
| subito pianissimo | f | a)  three strings; release the left (piano) pedal |
| senza pedale | j | b)  more spirited |
| lento | i | c)  smooth |
| adagio | k | d)  fast |
| presto | h | e)  with movement |
| più spiritoso | b | f)  suddenly very soft |
| allegro | d | g)  the same tempo |
| con moto | e | h)  very fast |
| tre corde | a | i)  slow |
| l'istesso tempo | g | j)  without pedal |
| | | k)  a slow tempo; slower than *andante* but not as slow as *largo* |

**9.** a) Name the key. Rewrite the following melody in the **ALTO** Clef at the **SAME PITCH**.

Key: _D Major_

b) Name the key. Rewrite the following melody in the **TENOR** Clef at the **SAME PITCH**.

Key: _D Major_

c) Name the key. Rewrite the following melody one octave **HIGHER** in the **TREBLE** Clef.

Key: _A Major_

**10.** Analyze the following piece of music by answering the questions below.

# Lonely Waltz

G. St. Germain

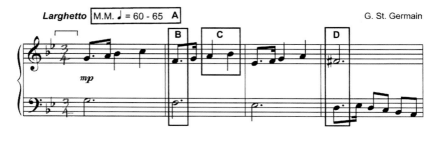

a) Add the correct Time Signature directly on the music.

b) Name the key of this piece. _g minor_

c) Explain the meaning at the letter **A**. _Maelzel's Metronome 60-65 quarter note beats per minute_

d) Name the intervals at the letters: **B** _Perfect 8_   **C** _minor 2_   **D** _Major 10_

e) Name the scale at the letter **E**. _g minor harmonic_

f) Circle one example of a tritone directly on the music. Name the interval: _diminished 5_

g) Circle the term for the relationship between mm. 1, 2 and 3.

        imitation     inversion     (sequence)

h) Circle the term for the relationship between the R.H. in m. 1 and the L.H. in m. 5.

        (imitation)     inversion     sequence

i) Name the type of cadence formed by the chords at the letter **F**. _Perfect_

j) Explain the meaning of **Larghetto.** _not as slow as largo (very slow)_

# Lesson 10   Scores - Short, Modern Vocal and String Quartet

A **SHORT SCORE** (Condensed score or Close score) is written for **FOUR** voices or instruments on two staves, Treble and Bass.  A short score may be written in Keyboard Style or Chorale Style.

**Keyboard Style**: Four part texture. Three notes in the Treble Clef and one note in the Bass Clef.

**Chorale Style**: Four part texture. Two notes in the Treble Clef and two notes in the Bass Clef.

♫ **Note:** The melody is written in the highest voice for both Keyboard Style and Chorale Style.

In **Chorale Style** the four parts (voices) are written with:
the UPPER notes in the Treble Clef, stems UP and the LOWER notes, stems DOWN.
the UPPER notes in the Bass Clef, stems UP and the LOWER notes, stems DOWN.

In **OPEN SCORE** each voice or instrument is written on its own staff, one above the other.  Notes are lined up vertically and normal stem rules apply.  A straight bracket is used to join the 4 staves.

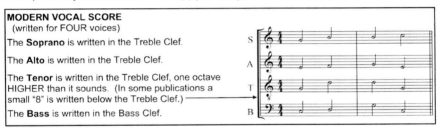

**MODERN VOCAL SCORE**
   (written for FOUR voices)

The **Soprano** is written in the Treble Clef.

The **Alto** is written in the Treble Clef.

The **Tenor** is written in the Treble Clef, one octave HIGHER than it sounds.  (In some publications a small "8" is written below the Treble Clef.)

The **Bass** is written in the Bass Clef.

1.  Name the 4 voices in the Modern Vocal Score:

   1. Soprano     2. Alto     3. Tenor     4. Bass

**STRING QUARTET SCORE**
   (written for FOUR instruments)

The **First Violin** (Vl.I) is written in the Treble Clef.

The **Second Violin** (Vl.II) is written in the Treble Clef.

The **Viola** (Vla.) is written in the Alto Clef.

The **Cello** (Vc.) is written in the Bass Clef.

2.  Name the 4 instruments in the String Quartet Score:

   1. First violin     2. Second violin     3. Viola     4. Cello

## REWRITING a SHORT SCORE into OPEN SCORE for MODERN VOCAL SCORE

**REWRITING a SHORT SCORE for MODERN VOCAL SCORE into OPEN SCORE Rules**:

**Title, Tempo and Composer**: written ONCE at the top of the score.
**Key Signature and Time Signature**: written at the beginning of each staff.
**Dynamics**: must be written ABOVE each staff where each voice begins when words are included.
**Fermata**: written ABOVE each staff.
**Bar Lines**: remain on the staff so as NOT to interfere with the words written below each staff.

♫ **Note:** Always use a ruler to keep all notes and bar lines vertical.

The **MODERN VOCAL SCORE** is a CHORAL Score written for FOUR voices: (SATB)
**Soprano** (Treble Clef),    **Alto** (Treble Clef),    **Tenor** (Treble Clef),    **Bass** (Bass Clef).

The **Short Score** is written on TWO staves that are joined
by a **BRACE** and a **LINE**. (Staves is the plural for Staff.)

The **Open Score** is written on FOUR staves that are
joined by a **BRACKET** and a **LINE**.

In Open Score for **Modern Vocal Score**, the four voices
(each written on its own staff) are in order of range from
highest to lowest. Normal stem rules apply.

In Short Score, the **Tenor** voice is written where it sounds.
In Open Score, the Tenor voice is written one octave
**HIGHER** than it sounds.

**O God, Our Help in Ages Past**

Brace, Line

1. Following the example, rewrite the Short Score above in Open Score for Modern Vocal Score.
   Name the four voices.

**O God, Our Help in Ages Past**

Bracket, Line

Voices:

Soprano

Alto

Tenor

Bass

## SHORT SCORE to MODERN VOCAL SCORE

In **SHORT SCORE**, a two note slur curves up in the Soprano and Tenor voices, and curves down in the Alto and Bass voices. Slurs are written in between the stems.
In **OPEN SCORE**, a two note slur is written on the notehead side when stems are in the same direction. For stems in opposite directions, the slur is written curved up in between the noteheads.

In **SHORT SCORE**, dotted line notes are written with the dot ABOVE the line in the Soprano and Tenor voices, and written with the dot BELOW the line in the Alto and Bass voices.
In **OPEN SCORE**, dotted line notes are written with the dot ABOVE the line.

♫ **Note:** An "excerpt" is a passage taken from a piece of music.

1. Rewrite the following excerpt in Open Score for Modern Vocal Score. Name the four voices.

115

**REWRITING a SHORT SCORE into OPEN SCORE for STRING QUARTET**

**REWRITING a SHORT SCORE for STRING QUARTET into Open Score Rules:**

**Title, Tempo and Composer:** written ONCE at the top of the score.
**Key Signature and Time Signature:** written at the beginning of each staff.
**Dynamics:** written BELOW each staff, starting with the first note.
**Fermata:** written ABOVE each staff.
**Bar Lines:** run continuously through all four staves.

♫ **Note:** Always use a ruler to keep all notes and barlines vertical.

The **STRING QUARTET** is an INSTRUMENTAL Score written for FOUR stringed instruments:

| **First Violin, Violin I** | **Second Violin, Violin II** | **Viola** | **Cello** |
|---|---|---|---|
| (Treble Clef) | (Treble Clef) | (Alto Clef) | (Bass Clef) |

The **Short Score** is written on TWO staves. If the same note is played by two instruments at the same time, it is given two stems; one up and one down.

In **String Quartet Score** the four instruments (each written on its own staff) each have their own notes. Normal stem rules apply.

In **Short Score**, staccato dots are written: ABOVE the stem for notes with stems up and BELOW the stem for notes with stems down.

1. Following the example, rewrite the Short Score above in Open Score for String Quartet. Name the four instruments.

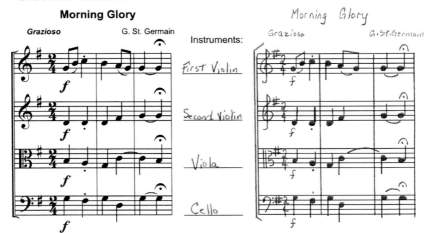

Instruments:

First Violin

Second Violin

Viola

Cello

# SHORT SCORE to STRING QUARTET

In **SHORT SCORE**, rests may be written higher or lower than usual on the staff depending on which instrument or voice is having a rest. Rests may also be written outside the staff (use ledger lines for breve, whole rest and half rests). When BOTH instruments or voices written in the SAME staff have the same rest, only ONE rest is written for both instruments or voices.

In **OPEN SCORE** each instrument or voice has its own rest. Correct placement of rest rules apply.

1. Rewrite the following excerpt in Open Score for String Quartet. Name the four instruments.

## REWRITING an OPEN SCORE into SHORT SCORE

**REWRITING an OPEN SCORE for Modern Vocal Score into SHORT SCORE Rules:**

**Short Score**: written on two staves, Treble and Bass. Stem direction identifies each voice.
**Soprano**: written in the Treble Clef, stems UP. **Alto**: written in the Treble Clef, stems DOWN.
**Tenor**: written in the Bass Clef, stems UP. **Bass**: written in the Bass Clef, stems DOWN.
If the same note is sung by two voices at the same time, it is given two stems: one up and one down.
**Words**: written in the middle of the Grand Staff.

**Fermata**: written ABOVE the soprano part and BELOW the bass part.
**Bar Lines**: remain on the staff and do NOT run continuously through both staves (as in piano music).

♫ **Note**: Always use a ruler to keep all notes and bar lines vertical.

In **SHORT SCORE**, the **BRACE** and bar line are written at the beginning of the staves.

1. Name the four voices. Rewrite the following excerpt in Short Score in Chorale Style.

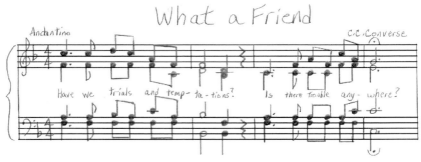

**OPEN SCORE to SHORT SCORE**

When rewriting an **OPEN SCORE** into **SHORT SCORE**, write the UPPER notes in the Treble Clef first. Use a ruler to line up the other notes directly below the top notes.

1. a) Name the type of Open Scores. Name the four voices or instruments for each.
   b) Rewrite the Open Scores into Short Scores in Chorale Style.

a) Type of Score: _String Quartet_               a) Type of Score: _Modern Vocal_

b) Short Score (of above)               b) Short Score (of above)

# Lesson 10      Review Test

Total Score: _____
100

Write the Circle of Fifths on a blank piece of paper. Use it as a reference when doing the review test.

1.  a) Write the following harmonic intervals **BELOW** the given notes. Use whole notes.

       Augmented 11      minor 6      Major 3      diminished 13      Perfect 12

    b) Invert the above intervals in the Bass Clef. Name the inversions.

     dim 5      Maj 3      min 6      Aug 3      Per 4

2.  Write the following seventh chords in the Treble Clef. Use whole notes. Use the correct Key Signature.

     a) the **DIMINISHED SEVENTH** chord of g sharp minor harmonic in root position
     b) the **DOMINANT SEVENTH** chord of B flat Major in second inversion
     c) the **DOMINANT SEVENTH** chord of c sharp minor harmonic in third inversion
     d) the **DOMINANT SEVENTH** chord of A Major in first inversion
     e) the **DIMINISHED SEVENTH** chord of e flat minor harmonic in root position

     a)      b)      c)      d)      e)

3.  Name each of the following chords as: Major triad, minor triad, Augmented triad, diminished triad, seventh chord, quartal chord, polychord or cluster chord.

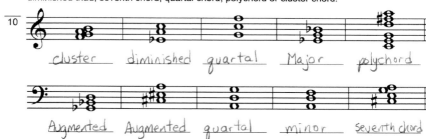

     cluster      diminished      quartal      Major      polychord

     Augmented      Augmented      quartal      minor      seventh chord

**4.** a) The following melody is written for Trumpet in B flat. Name the key in which it is written. Transpose it to concert pitch in the Treble Clef. Use the correct Key Signature. Name the new key.

Key: _A Major_

Key: _G Major_

b) Name the key of the following melody. Transpose it **DOWN** a diminished fourth in the Bass Clef. Use the correct key signature. Name the new key.

Key: _d minor_

Key: _a# minor_

**5.** Write the Basic Beat and the pulse below each measure. Add rests below each bracket to complete the measure. Cross off the Basic Beat as each beat is completed.

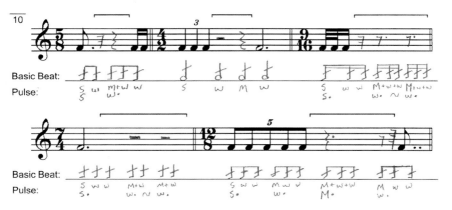

Basic Beat: _____

Pulse: _____

Basic Beat: _____

Pulse: _____

**6.** Write the following scales, ascending and descending, in the clefs indicated. Use whole notes. Use accidentals.

10  a) Whole tone scale starting on C sharp
    b) a flat minor melodic, from Submediant to Submediant
    c) enharmonic Tonic Major of b minor
    d) chromatic scale starting on E
    e) Lydian mode starting on C flat
    f) g sharp minor harmonic, from Subdominant to Subdominant

a)
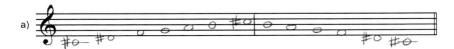

b)
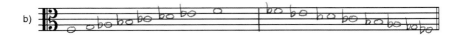

c)
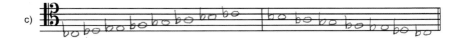

d)
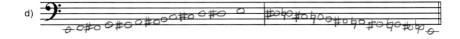

e)
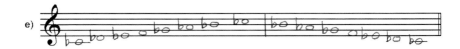

f)
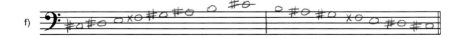

**7.** a) Name the key for the following melodic fragments. Use chord symbols to identify the cadence. Write a cadence (keyboard style) **BELOW** the bracketed notes. Name the type of cadence (Perfect, Plagal or Imperfect).

10

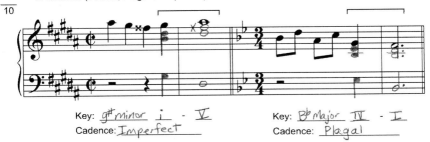

Key: _g# minor_ _i_ - _V_
Cadence: _Imperfect_

Key: _Bb Major_ _IV_ - _I_
Cadence: _Plagal_

b) Name the key for each of the following cadences. Use chord symbols to identify the cadence. Name the type of cadence (Perfect, Plagal or Imperfect).

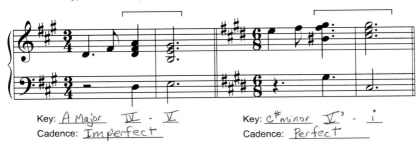

Key: _A Major_ _IV_ - _V_
Cadence: _Imperfect_

Key: _c# minor_ _V⁷_ - _i_
Cadence: _Perfect_

**8.** Match each musical term or sign with its English definition. (Not all definitions will be used.)

10

| Term | | Definition |
|------|------|------------|
| da capo, D.C. | _h_ | a) from the sign, 𝄋 |
| dal segno, D.S. | _a_ | b) play one octave above the written pitch |
| D.C. al Fine | _f_ | c) hold for the combined value of the tied notes |
| ⌢ | _k_ | d) Maelzel's metronome |
| Tempo primo, Tempo I | _e_ | e) return to the original tempo |
| M.M. | _d_ | f) repeat from the beginning and end at *Fine* |
| 8va- - - ⌟ | _·_ _j_ | g) repeat the music within the double bars |
| 8va- - - ⌝ | _b_ | h) from the beginning |
| ♩ ♩ | _c_ | i) accent, a stressed note |
| (staff) | _g_ | j) play one octave below the written pitch |
| | | k) fermata, pause; hold the note or rest longer than its written value |

123

**9.** a) Name the type of Open Score below: <u>String Quartet</u>

b) Name the four voices or instruments for the score below. (Do not use abbreviations.)

10

<u>First Violin</u>     <u>Second Violin</u>     <u>Viola</u>     <u>Cello</u>

c) Rewrite the following excerpt in Short Score in Chorale Style (using the two staves below).

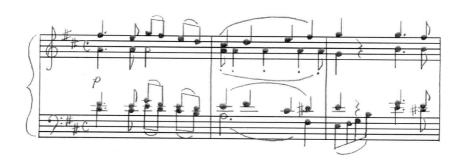

124

**10.** Analyze the following excerpt by answering the questions below.

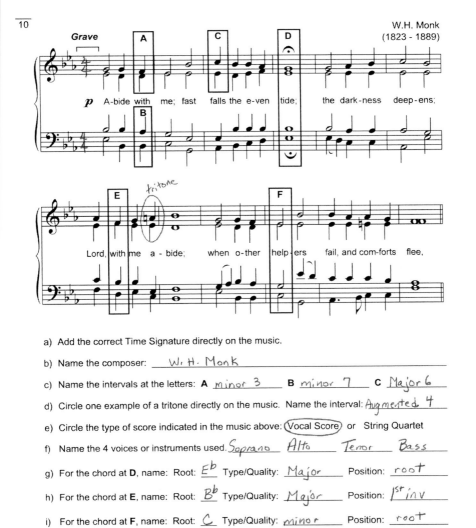

a) Add the correct Time Signature directly on the music.

b) Name the composer: ___W. H. Monk___

c) Name the intervals at the letters: **A** _minor 3_ **B** _minor 7_ **C** _Major 6_

d) Circle one example of a tritone directly on the music. Name the interval: _Augmented 4_

e) Circle the type of score indicated in the music above: (Vocal Score) or String Quartet

f) Name the 4 voices or instruments used. _Soprano_ _Alto_ _Tenor_ _Bass_

g) For the chord at **D**, name: Root: _E♭_ Type/Quality: _Major_ Position: _root_

h) For the chord at **E**, name: Root: _B♭_ Type/Quality: _Major_ Position: _1st inv_

i) For the chord at **F**, name: Root: _C_ Type/Quality: _minor_ Position: _root_

j) Explain the meaning of **Grave**. _Slow and solemn_

# Lesson 11     Analysis - Musical Compositions

**ANALYSIS** of a piece of music develops a deeper understanding of the composers ideas.

1. Analyze the following piece of music by answering the questions below.

a) The **COMPOSER'S** name is written at the top right of the piece. The dates underneath are the year of his/her birth and death. If there is only one date, it is the year of birth and the composer is still alive.

Name the composer. Domenico Scarlatti     When did he/she live? 1685-1757

b) When naming the **KEY**, look at the Key Signature. Check for the raised 7th note of the harmonic minor key to determine if the key is Major or minor. The piece will often end on the Tonic.

Name the Key: d minor     Tonic: D     Dominant: A     Leading note: C#

c) When writing the **TIME SIGNATURE** on the music, always write it in BOTH clefs. Look at several measures to determine if there is a pickup beat (anacrusis or incomplete measure).

Write the Time Signature directly on the music.

The **TEMPO** is written directly above the Time Signature.

Name and explain the tempo of this piece. Andante - moderately slow, at a walking pace

d) When counting the number of **MEASURES** in a piece, a repeat sign WILL NOT affect the number of measures.

How many measures are in this piece?     8

When all repeat signs are observed, how many measures of music are played?     16

Measure numbers may be written in a small square at the beginning of each line of music.

Write the measure number in the square at the letter **A**.

e) When naming a chord, the **ROOT** is determined by the lowest note when in root position. The **TYPE/QUALITY** of a chord may be a Major, minor, Augmented or diminished triad; or a Dominant seventh ($V^7$) or diminished seventh ($vii^{o7}$) chord. The chord is determined by the intervals above the Root. The **POSITION**, root position, first inversion, second inversion or third inversion (for seventh chords), is determined by the lowest note. Name the chord at the following letters:

**B**: Root: _A_   Type/Quality: _Dominant 7th_   Position: _3rd inv_

**C**: Root: _D_   Type/Quality: _minor_   Position: _1st inv_

f) When identifying **INTERVALS**, count ALL the lines and ALL the spaces. Check the Key Signature, changes in clefs and any accidentals in the measure that would affect the note.

Circle and label a tritone directly on the music. Name the interval. _m.2 - dim 5 , m.5 - Aug 4_

Name the intervals at the following letters: **D**: _minor 2_   **E**: _Major 2_   **F**: _minor 13_

g) When adding a **REST(S)** to complete a measure, determine the Time Signature and follow the rest rules.

Write the appropriate rest(s) at the letter **G**. Name the type of rest used. _eighth rest_

h) When analyzing an **OPEN SCORE**, check the clef signs to determine if it is written for Modern Vocal Score or String Quartet.

Is this piece written in open score or closed score for piano? _closed score for piano_

Name the clefs and voices/instruments for each of the following open scores. _*written one octave higher than it sounds_

Modern Vocal Score
Clef: _Treble_   _Treble_   _*Treble_   _Bass_

Voice/Instrument: _Soprano_   _Alto_   _Tenor_   _Bass_

String Quartet
Clef: _Treble_   _Treble_   _Alto_   _Bass_

Voice/Instrument: _First Violin_   _Second Violin_   _Viola_   _Cello_

i) Determining the relationship of the motive (musical idea or phrase) and other measures, look for:
**IMITATION** - the motive is repeated by another voice/instrument at the same or different pitch.
**INVERSION** - the motive is turned "upside-down". Interval directions (up or down) are reversed.
**SEQUENCE** - the motive is repeated (one or more times) at a higher or lower pitch.

Give the term for the relationship in the R.H between mm. 1 - 2 and mm. 3 - 4. _Sequence_

j) When identifying a **CADENCE** as Perfect, Plagal or Imperfect, determine the key. Count UP from the Tonic note to determine the degree of the bass notes. Look for the raised 7th note of the harmonic minor key.

Name the cadence at the letter **H**. _Perfect_

# Lesson 11　　　　　　Review Test

Total Score: ____

100

Write the Circle of Fifths on a blank piece of paper. Use it as a reference when doing the review test.

**1.** a) Name the following harmonic intervals.

10

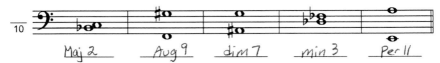

Maj 2　　　Aug 9　　　dim 7　　　min 3　　　Per 11

b) Invert the above intervals in the Treble Clef. Use whole notes. Name the inversions.

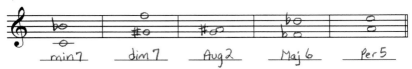

min 7　　　dim 7　　　Aug 2　　　Maj 6　　　Per 5

**2.** Write the following triads using accidentals. Use whole notes. Name the type/quality (Major, minor, Augmented or diminished).

　　a) the **LEADING NOTE** triad of c minor harmonic in first inversion

10　　b) the **SUPERTONIC** triad of C Major in root position

　　c) the **TONIC** triad of f minor harmonic in second inversion

　　d) the **DOMINANT** triad of D flat Major in first inversion

　　e) the **MEDIANT** triad of c minor harmonic in root position

　　f) Name the scale which contains all of these chords: ___C minor harmonic___

Type: ___dim___　___min___　___min___　___Maj___　___Aug___

**3.** For each of the following seventh chords, name:

　　a) the key to which each chord belongs (Major or minor).

　　b) the type (Dominant seventh, $V^7$, or diminished seventh, $vii^{o7}$).

10　　c) the position (root, 1st inversion, 2nd inversion or 3rd inversion).

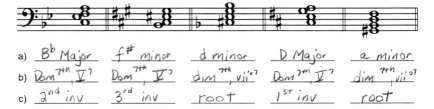

a) ___Bb Major___　___f# minor___　___d minor___　___D Major___　___a minor___

b) ___Dom 7th, V7___　___Dom 7th, V7___　___dim 7th, vii°7___　___Dom 7th, V7___　___dim 7th, vii°7___

c) ___2nd inv___　___3rd inv___　___root___　___1st inv___　___root___

**4.** a) The following melody is written for French Horn in F. Name the key in which it is written. Transpose it to concert pitch in the Bass Clef. Use the correct Key Signature. Name the new key.

Key: _Bb Major_

Key: _Eb Major_

b) Transpose the given melody **DOWN** a diminished fourth in the Bass Clef. Use the correct Key Signature. Name the new key.

Key: _F# Major_

**5.** Write the Basic Beat and the pulse below each measure. Add rests below each bracket to complete the measure. Cross off the Basic Beat as each beat is completed.

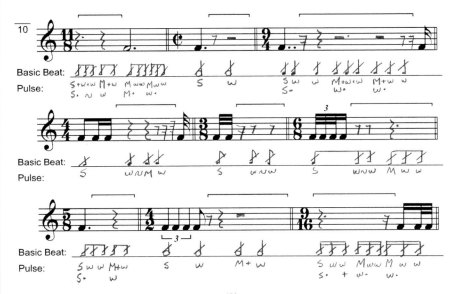

129

**6.** Write the following scales, ascending and descending, in the clefs indicated. Use whole notes.

    a) whole tone scale starting on E using any standard notation

10  b) a sharp minor melodic, from Leading note to Leading note, using the correct Key Signature

    c) b flat minor harmonic, from Subdominant to Subdominant, using the correct Key Signature

    d) Phrygian mode starting on A sharp using accidentals

    e) enharmonic relative minor, melodic form, of C flat Major using accidentals

    f) Dorian mode starting on C using accidentals

a)

b)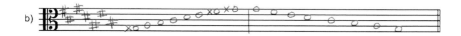

c)

d)

e)

f)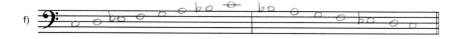

**7.** a) Name the key for the following melodic fragments. Use chord symbols to identify the cadence. Write a cadence (keyboard style) **BELOW** the bracketed notes. Name the type of cadence (Perfect, Plagal or Imperfect).

10

Key: b♭ minor    iv - i
Cadence: Plagal

Key: e minor    iv - V
Cadence: Imperfect

b) Name the key for each of the following cadences. Use chord symbols to identify the cadence. Name the type of cadence (Perfect, Plagal or Imperfect).

Key: C♭ Major    V⁷ - I
Cadence: Perfect

Key: g minor    i - V
Cadence: Imperfect

**8.** Match each musical term with its English definition. (Not all definitions will be used.)

| | Term | | Definition |
|---|---|---|---|
| 10 | mässig | f | a) with expression |
| | sehr schnell | j | b) slow, slowly |
| | mit Ausdruck | a | c) marked or stressed |
| | quasi | i | d) less movement, slower |
| | langsam | b | e) lively, brisk |
| | marcato, marc. | c | f) moderate, moderately |
| | meno mosso | d | g) with mute |
| | ritenuto, riten. | k | h) with spirit |
| | con sordino | g | i) almost, as if |
| | vivace | e | j) very fast |
| | | | k) suddenly slower, held back |

**9.**　a) Name the four voices or instruments for the following **OPEN** Scores. (Do not use abbreviations.)

Modern Vocal Score: <u>Soprano</u>　<u>Alto</u>　<u>Tenor</u>　<u>Bass</u>

String Quartet: 　<u>First Violin</u> <u>Second Violin</u>　<u>Viola</u>　<u>Cello</u>

b) Rewrite the excerpt in **OPEN** Score for each of the following:

**Modern Vocal Score**　　　　　　　　**String Quartet**

**10.** Analyze the following piece of music by answering the questions below.

# Friday Night

*Scherzando*

G. St. Germain

a) Add the correct Time Signature directly on the music.

b) Name the key of this piece. ___C minor___

c) Name the composer. ___G. St. Germain___

d) Name the intervals at the letters: **A** ___Aug 1___   **B** ___min 3___   **C** ___Per 15___

e) Explain the relationship between the RH in measure 5 and 6. ___inversion___

f) For the chord at **D**, name: Root: ___G___ Type/Quality: ___minor___ Position: ___2nd inv___

g) For the chord at **E**, name: Root: ___D___ Type/Quality: ___dim___ Position: ___root___

h) Name the type of scale at the letter **F**. ___blues___

i) Name the type of cadence at the letter **G**. ___Perfect___

j) Explain the meaning of *Scherzando*. ___playful___

# Lesson 12    Musical Terms, Definitions and Signs

**MUSICAL TERMS** and **SIGNS** (usually in Italian) indicate tempo, changes in tempo, pedal, articulation, dynamics and style in performance. Terms may also be written in German or French.

## TEMPO, CHANGES in TEMPO and PEDAL

| Tempo | Definition |
|---|---|
| *adagio* | a slow tempo (slower than *andante* but not as slow as *largo*) |
| *allegretto* | fairly fast (a little slower than *allegro*) |
| *allegro* | fast |
| *andante* | moderately slow; at a walking pace |
| *andantino* | a little faster than *andante* |
| *comodo* | at a comfortable, easy tempo |
| *con moto* | with movement |
| *grave* | slow and solemn |
| *larghetto* | not as slow as *largo* |
| *largo* | very slow |
| *lento* | slow |
| *moderato* | at a moderate tempo |
| *presto* | very fast |
| *prestissimo* | as fast as possible |
| *stringendo* | pressing, becoming faster |
| *vivace* | lively, brisk |

| Changes in Tempo | Definition |
|---|---|
| *accelerando, accel.* | becoming quicker |
| *allargando, allarg.* | broadening, becoming slower |
| *a tempo* | return to the original tempo |
| *calando* | becoming slower and softer |
| *l'istesso tempo* | the same tempo |
| *meno mosso* | less movement, slower |
| *più mosso* | more movement, quicker |
| *rallentando, rall.* | slowing down |
| *ritardando, rit.* | slowing down gradually |
| *ritenuto, riten.* | suddenly slower, held back |
| *rubato* | with some freedom of tempo to enhance musical expression |
| *Tempo primo, Tempo I* | return to the original tempo |

| Pedal | Definition |
|---|---|
| *pedale, ped* | pedal |
| *con pedale,* 🎵 | with pedal |
| *tre corde* | three strings; release the left (piano) pedal |
| *una corda* | one string; depress the left (piano) pedal |
| └─────┘ | pedal marking |

1. Give the Italian term for each of the following definitions:

<u>Comodo</u>                    <u>calando</u>                    <u>una  corda</u>
at a comfortable, easy tempo    becoming slower and softer    one string; depress the left pedal

# ARTICULATION, DYNAMICS and ITALIAN TERMS

| Articulation | Definition | Sign |
|---|---|---|
| marcato, marc. | marked or stressed | |
| martellato | strongly accented, hammered | |
| accent | a stressed note | |
| pesante | weighty, with emphasis | |
| legato | smooth | |
| slur | play the notes legato | |
| leggiero | light, nimble, quick | |
| staccato | detached | |
| sostenuto | sustained | |
| tenuto | held, sustained | |

| Dynamics | Definition |
|---|---|
| crescendo, cresc. | becoming louder |
| decrescendo, decresc. | becoming softer |
| diminuendo, dim. | becoming softer |
| forte, f | loud |
| fortepiano, fp | loud, then suddenly soft |
| fortissimo, ff | very loud |
| mezzo forte, mf | moderately loud |
| mezzo piano, mp | moderately soft |
| piano, p | soft |
| pianissimo, pp | very soft |
| sforzando, sf, sfz | a sudden strong accent of a single note or chord |

| Italian Terms | Definition |
|---|---|
| arco | for stringed instruments: resume bowing after a pizzicato passage |
| attacca | proceed without a break |
| con sordino | with mute |
| fine | the end |
| loco | return to normal register |
| ottava, 8va | the interval of an octave |
| pizzicato | for stringed instruments:  pluck the string instead of bowing |
| primo, prima | first; the upper part of a duet |
| quindicesima alta (15ma) | two octaves higher |
| risoluto | resolute |
| secondo, seconda | second; second or lower part of a duet |
| simile | continue in the same manner as has just been indicated |
| tacet | be silent |
| tempo | speed at which music is performed |
| tutti | a passage for the ensemble |
| volta | time (for example, prima volta, first time; seconda volta, second time) |
| volti subito, v.s. | turn the page quickly |

1. Give the Italian term for each of the following definitions:

   <u>martellato</u>          <u>fortepiano, fp</u>          <u>attacca</u>
   strongly accented, hammered      loud, then suddenly soft      proceed without a break

## PREFIX and SIGNS

| Prefix | Definition |
|---|---|
| *alla, all'* | in the manner of |
| *assai* | much, very much |
| *ben, bene* | well |
| *col, coll', colla, colle* | with |
| *con* | with |
| *e, ed* | and |
| *ma* | but |
| *meno* | less |
| *molto* | much, very |
| *non* | not |
| *non troppo* | not too much |
| *più* | more |
| *poco* | little |
| *poco a poco* | little by little |
| *quasi* | almost, as if |
| *sempre* | always, continuously |
| *senza* | without |
| *sopra* | above |
| *subito* | suddenly |
| *troppo* | too much |

| Signs | Definition |
|---|---|
| D.C. al Fine | repeat from the beginning and end at *Fine* |
| D.C. | *da capo*, from the beginning |
| 𝄋 | *dal segno, D.S.,* from the sign |
| 𝄐 | *fermata*: a pause; hold the note or rest longer than its written value |
| M.D. | *mano destra*, right hand |
| M.S. | *mano sinistra*, left hand |
| M.M. | Maelzel's metronome |
| $8^{va}$- - - ⌐ *ottava,* $8^{va}$ | play one octave above the written pitch |
| $8^{va}$- - - ⌐ *ottava,* $8^{va}$ | play one octave below the written pitch |
| 𝄆 𝄇 | *repeat signs*: repeat the music within the double bars |
| ♩ ♩ | *tie*: hold for the combined value of the tied notes |

1. Give the Italian term or sign for each of the following definitions:

| <u>subito</u> | <u>sopra</u> | <u>D.C., da capo</u> | <u>M.S. mano sinistra</u> |
|---|---|---|---|
| suddenly | above | from the beginning | left hand |

# STYLE in PERFORMANCE, FRENCH TERMS and GERMAN TERMS

| Style in Performance | Definition |
|---|---|
| *ad libitum, ad lib.* | at the liberty of the performer |
| *agitato* | agitated |
| *animato* | lively, animated |
| *brillante* | brilliant |
| *cantabile* | in a singing style |
| *con brio* | with vigor, spirit |
| *con espressione* | with expression |
| *con fuoco* | with fire |
| *con grazia* | with grace |
| *dolce* | sweet, gentle |
| *dolente* | sad |
| *espressivo, espress.* | expressive, with expression |
| *giocoso* | humorous, jocose |
| *grandioso* | grand, grandiose |
| *grazioso* | graceful |
| *largamente* | broadly |
| *maestoso* | majestic |
| *mesto* | sad, mournful |
| *morendo* | dying, fading away |
| *scherzando* | playful |
| *semplice* | simple |
| *sonore* | sonorous |
| *sotto voce* | soft, subdued, under the breath |
| *spiritoso* | spirited |
| *tranquillo* | quiet, tranquil |
| *vivo* | lively |

| French Term | Definition |
|---|---|
| *cédez* | yield; hold the tempo back |
| *léger* | light; lightly |
| *lentement* | slowly |
| *modéré* | at a moderate tempo |
| *mouvement* | tempo; motion |
| *vite* | fast |

| German Term | Definition |
|---|---|
| *bewegt* | moving |
| *langsam* | slow, slowly |
| *mässig* | moderate, moderately |
| *mit Ausdruck* | with expression |
| *sehr* | very |
| *schnell* | fast |

1. Give the term in Italian, French and German for the following definition:

<u>lento</u>    <u>lente ment</u>    <u>langsam</u>
slow (Italian)       slowly (French)       slow, slowly (German)

# REVIEW: ULTIMATE MUSIC THEORY - ADVANCED GUIDE and CHART

1. Complete the following to create the Ultimate Music Theory Guide and Chart - Advanced.

## Circle of Fifths

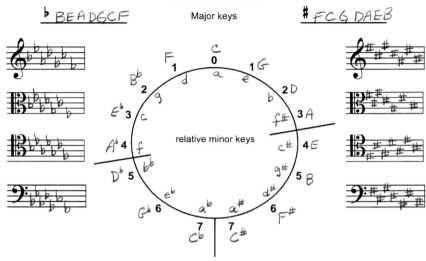

| Scale Degree: | Technical Name: | Hint: | Mode: |
|---|---|---|---|
| 1̂ | Tonic | I | Ionian |
| 2̂ | Supertonic | Do | Dorian |
| 3̂ | Mediant | Play | Phrygian |
| 4̂ | Subdominant | Like | Lydian |
| 5̂ | Dominant | Mozart | Mixolydian |
| 6̂ | Submediant | And | Aeolian |
| 7̂ | Leading note | Liszt | Locrian |

**OPEN SCORES:**

**String Quartet**

| First Violin | Treble Clef |
|---|---|
| Second Violin | Treble Clef |
| Viola | Alto Clef |
| Cello | Bass Clef |

**Modern Vocal**

| Soprano | Treble Clef |
|---|---|
| Alto | Treble Clef |
| Tenor | Treble Clef |
| Bass | Bass Clef |

**Transposing to Concert Pitch:**

Trumpet in B♭ and Clarinet in B♭: Down a Major 2

English Horn and French Horn in F: Down a Perfect 5

**Chords - Type/Quality:**

| | Major | Dom 7th | minor | Augmented | diminished | dim 7th |
|---|---|---|---|---|---|---|
| Interval above the Root: | | min 7 | | | | dim 7 |
| Interval above the Root: | Per 5 | Per 5 | Per 5 | Aug 5 | dim 5 | dim 5 |
| Interval above the Root: | Maj 3 | Maj 3 | min 3 | Maj 3 | min 3 | min 3 |

138

# Lesson 12     **Final Advanced Exam**

Total Score: _____
100

Write the Circle of Fifths on a blank piece of paper.  Use it as a reference when doing the review test.

**1.**  a) Name the following intervals.

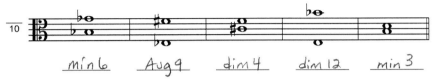

min 6    Aug 9    dim 4    dim 12    min 3

b) Invert the above intervals in the Treble Clef.  Name the inversions.

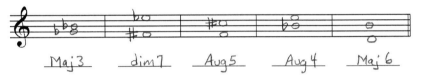

Maj 3    dim 7    Aug 5    Aug 4    Maj 6

**2.**  For each of the following seventh chords, name:
  a) the key to which each chord belongs (Major or minor).
  b) the type (Dominant seventh, $V^7$, or diminished seventh, $vii^{o7}$).
  c) the position (root, 1st inversion, 2nd inversion or 3rd inversion).

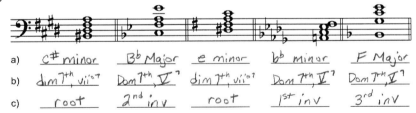

a)  c# minor    Bb Major    e minor    bb minor    F Major

b)  dim 7th, vii°7    Dom 7th, V 7    dim 7th, vii°7    Dom 7th, V 7    Dom 7th, V 7

c)  root    2nd inv    root    1st inv    3rd inv

**3.**  Name the following for each of the triads below:
  a) the Root.
  b) the type/quality (Major, minor, Augmented or diminished).
  c) the position (root position, 1st inversion or 2nd inversion).

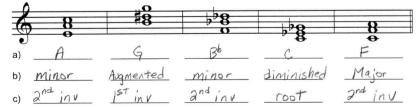

a)  A    G    Bb    C    F

b)  minor    Augmented    minor    diminished    Major

c)  2nd inv    1st inv    2nd inv    root    2nd inv

**4.** a) The following melody is written for Trumpet in B flat. Name the key in which it is written. Transpose it to concert pitch in the Bass Clef. Use the correct Key Signature. Name the new key.

Key: _Ab Major_

Key: _Gb Major_

b) Transpose the given melody **DOWN** a minor sixth in the Bass Clef. Use the correct Key Signature. Name the new key.

Key: _C Major_

**5.** Write the Basic Beat and the pulse below each measure. Add rests below each bracket to complete the measure. Cross off the Basic Beat as each beat is completed.

140

**6.** Write the following scales, ascending and descending, in the clefs indicated.  Use whole notes.

a) B Major, from Supertonic to Supertonic, using the correct Key Signature
10 b) f minor melodic, from Leading note to Leading note, using the correct Key Signature
c) enharmonic Tonic minor, harmonic form, of g sharp minor using accidentals
d) Mixolydian mode starting on F using any standard notation

a)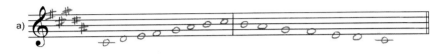

b)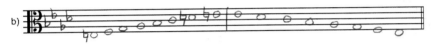

c)

d)

e) Identify the following scales as Major pentatonic, minor pentatonic, octatonic, blues, whole tone or chromatic.

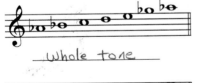

_whole tone_

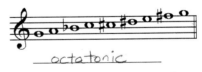

_octatonic_

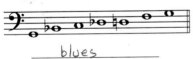

_blues_

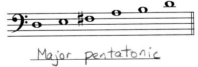

_Major pentatonic_

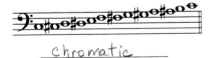

_chromatic_

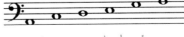

_minor pentatonic_

**7.**   a) Name the key for the following melodic fragments.  Use chord symbols to identify the
cadence.  Write a cadence (keyboard style) **BELOW** the bracketed notes.  Name the type
of cadence (Perfect, Plagal or Imperfect).

10

Key: F♯ Major   IV - V          Key: d♯ minor  V - i
Cadence: Imperfect              Cadence: Perfect

b) Name the key for each of the following cadences.  Use chord symbols to identify the cadence.
Name the type of cadence (Perfect, Plagal or Imperfect).

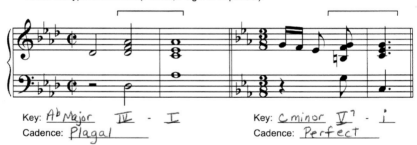

Key: A♭ Major   IV - I          Key: C minor   V⁷ - i
Cadence: Plagal                 Cadence: Perfect

**8.**   Match each musical term with its English definition.  (Not all definitions will be used.)

10

| Term | | Definition |
|------|------|------------|
| a tempo | f | a)  be silent |
| bewegt | g | b)  slow, slowly |
| tacet | a | c)  dying, fading away |
| mässig | i | d)  always, continuously |
| langsam | b | e)  fairly fast (a little slower than *allegro*) |
| morendo | c | f)  return to the original tempo |
| sempre | d | g)  moving |
| coll' ottava | j | h)  becoming faster |
| allegretto | e | i)  moderate, moderately |
| fine | k | j)  with an added octave |
| | | k)  the end |

142

**9.** Rewrite the following excerpt in Open Score for String Quartet. Name the four instruments.

First Violin

Second Violin

Viola

Cello

**10.** Analyze the following piece by answering the questions below.

# Blue Melody

R. St. Germain
G. St. Germain

*Dolce, con espressione*

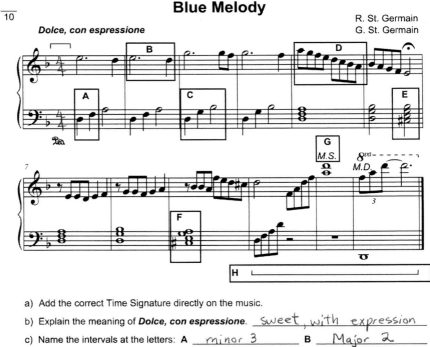

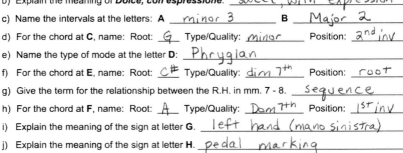

a) Add the correct Time Signature directly on the music.

b) Explain the meaning of **Dolce, con espressione**. _Sweet, with expression_

c) Name the intervals at the letters: **A** _minor 3_     **B** _Major 2_

d) For the chord at **C**, name: Root: _G_ Type/Quality: _minor_ Position: _2nd inv_

e) Name the type of mode at the letter **D**: _Phrygian_

f) For the chord at **E**, name: Root: _C#_ Type/Quality: _dim 7th_ Position: _root_

g) Give the term for the relationship between the R.H. in mm. 7 - 8. _sequence_

h) For the chord at **F**, name: Root: _A_ Type/Quality: _Dom 7th_ Position: _1st inv_

i) Explain the meaning of the sign at letter **G**. _left hand (mano sinistra)_

j) Explain the meaning of the sign at letter **H**. _pedal marking_

UltimateMusicTheory.com